P9-BZE-998

bastards

bastards

a memoir

MARY ANNA KING

W. W. NORTON & COMPANY

New York ~ *London*

For
Jacob, Becca, Lisa, Rebekah, Meghan, & Lesley
I love you, Bananas.

Copyright © 2015 by Mary Anna King
Frontis photograph from author's personal collection

All rights reserved
Printed in the United States of America
First Edition

For information about permission to reproduce selections from this book,
write to Permissions, W. W. Norton & Company, Inc.,
500 Fifth Avenue, New York, NY 10110

For information about special discounts for bulk purchases, please contact
W. W. Norton Special Sales at specialsales@wwnorton.com or 800-233-4830

Manufacturing by Courier Westford
Book design by Fearn Cutler de Vicq
Production managers: Ruth Toda and Devon Zahn

Library of Congress Cataloging-in-Publication Data

King, Mary Anna.
Bastards : a memoir / Mary Anna King. — First edition.
pages cm
Summary: "'A stirring, vividly told story of a young woman's quest to find the family she lost . . .
an impressive debut'-Peter Balakian; Born into poverty in southern New Jersey and raised in a com-
mune of single mothers, Mary Anna King watched her mother give away one of her newborn sisters
every year to another family. All told, there were seven children: Mary, her older brother, and five
phantom sisters. Then one day, Mary was sent away, too. Living in Oklahoma with her maternal
grandfather, Mary gets a new name and a new life. But she's haunted by the past: by the baby girls
she's sure will come looking for her someday, by the mother she had to leave behind, by the father
who left her. Mary is a college student when her sisters start to get back in touch. With each reunion,
her family becomes closer to whole again. Moving, haunting, and at times wickedly funny, Bastards
is about finding one's family and oneself"—Provided by publisher.
ISBN 978-0-393-08861-8 (hardcover)
1. King, Mary Anna—Family. 2. King, Mary Anna—Childhood and youth. 3. Young women—
United States—Biography. 4. Children of single parents—New Jersey—Biography. 5. Poor
families—New Jersey—Biography. 6. Sisters—United States—Biography. 7. Family reunions—
United States. 8. New Jersey—Biography. 9. Oklahoma—Biography. I. Title.
CT275.K5648A3 2005
306.8509749—dc23
2014047961

W. W. Norton & Company, Inc.
500 Fifth Avenue, New York, N.Y. 10110
www.wwnorton.com

W. W. Norton & Company Ltd.
Castle House, 75/76 Wells Street, London W1T 3QT

1 2 3 4 5 6 7 8 9 0

Contents

PART THREE: FOUND

Note

To write this book I consulted my personal journals from my childhood. I spoke with my sisters, brother, mothers, and father, who lived through certain bits of it alongside me, though these are the events as I recall them.

When necessary, time frames have been condensed, though only when doing so would not compromise the underlying truth of the narrative. One minor character is a composite. Many names have been changed.

bastards

Prologue
2009

R emember . . . the last sense you lose is your hearing."
My friend on the other side of the phone is a veteran intensive care nurse, so she ought to know.

"As long as she is breathing, she can hear you."

I nod into the phone and wait for someone to helpfully shout into the receiver, *She's nodding*, like my brother did once when we were kids. But I am standing in an airport departure gate where I am just another stranger on a cell phone, another transient whom no one will remember. My nurse friend's voice drops into the woolly alto register of one accustomed to soothing other people.

"Don't be surprised if it goes quickly . . . once she realizes that everyone is there."

"Okay."

It's New Year's Eve, and I'm headed to Oklahoma because my mother is dying.

I keep repeating that phrase—my mother is dying—although it isn't quite true. I say "my mother," because that is what people will understand. *My mother is dying* was what I said to my boss when I called him from the cab on the way to the airport, so it would be easy for him to comprehend, so the appropriate proto-

3

cols could be observed. But Mimi is not the woman who raised me all my life. She could have been, but she wasn't. It is that arbitrariness that has led me to struggle for as long as I can remember to reconcile the person I am with the one I might have been.

As I board my plane in Los Angeles, my brother, Jacob, begins his drive to Oklahoma from south Texas, where he is stationed with the U.S. Army. When my plane lands in Dallas for a two-hour layover, he is my first phone call. On paper, Jacob is in fact my *nephew*, but to call my brother my nephew is surreal and inconceivable. "I'm a mile away, I'm coming to get you," he says in his New Jersey drawl. In another life I had that accent, too.

I slip into the passenger seat of Jacob's beige sedan and we drive into the worst ice storm that has hit the center of the country in one hundred years.

"Mind if I smoke?" he asks.

"Not if you give me one, too."

He smirks and hands me the cigarette he just lit, pulling one for himself from the pack in the cup holder. We leave a trail of smoke as we drive up Interstate 35, unimpeded except for the occasional patch of black ice. Local newscasters' crowing about the Storm of the Century has kept most other drivers off the road tonight. That and the fact that it's New Year's Eve. Most people in the Interstate 35 corridor from Dallas to Oklahoma City are at parties, drinking champagne and waiting for balls to drop. Mimi gave me my first sip of champagne on a New Year's Eve seventeen years ago. I was ten years old and we were waiting to watch the fireworks over downtown Oklahoma City. She handed me a saucerlike glass with a sparkling pink liquid in it—half champagne and half strawberry Nehi soda. It was sweet and bitter and the bubbles made me sneeze.

I ask Jacob what he remembers about Oklahoma, the few

years that he lived there with me, our sister Rebecca, Granddad, and Mimi. "Nothing," he says. He clicks the radio dial to find a station that will stay free of static. We smoke two more cigarettes. We're in the flat middle of the country. There is nothing to block the frigid wind whistling over our windshield.

When we get to Oklahoma City, we loop around the Will Rogers World Airport until Rebecca arrives from Minneapolis. It's after ten o'clock at night by the time the three of us arrive in the intensive care unit at Baptist Hospital. Granddad is in the room with Mimi when we arrive, just as he has been since Christmas Day when she was admitted. Seventeen years ago—when Granddad became, on paper, my father—I was afraid of him, afraid of the way he could turn so quickly from the guy who sang Irving Berlin songs to wake us up in the morning to a red-faced, jaw-clenching belt-wielder. He is seventy-six now. His shoulders have rounded and he has softened.

Rebecca and I hug him and Jacob shakes his hand. "We'll take the night shift," I say to him. There's a moment when all four of us look at the unconscious Mimi and listen to the sound of her breathing. It's loud and fuzzy, an aircraft engine preparing for takeoff.

I tell Granddad what my nurse friend said on the phone, that the last sense you lose is your hearing, because I need to say something and there is nothing else to say.

He nods, and tells me he'll be back in the morning.

Many people have an event that tears their lives into before and after. Before the divorce and after the divorce. Before the war and after the war; before 9/11 and after 9/11. If I were like most people, Mimi's death—my mother's death—would have been that event for me. But in fact, losing people is the only constant I know.

PART ONE

jersey

1983–1989

The Day the Music Died

At the end of summer in 1983, I was fourteen months old, Jacob was two years, and Rebecca, whom we called Becky Jo, was two months. She was born the day after my first birthday: my only present that year. Our daddy worked construction and deejayed weddings on the weekends. Mom had been a cashier at a department store until she quit to stay home with us kids. We lived in a one-bedroom apartment in southern New Jersey, just outside of Philadelphia. My parents had been married four years. They were young. Their passions burned like an incinerator and swung wildly from love to hate and back again.

UNCLE MAC was my daddy's little brother, the baby of his family. He had been the best man at my parents' wedding in 1979, and would be Becky Jo's godfather when she was baptized. At twenty, he was a pink-cheeked homebody with a sweet singing voice and a mop of jet-black hair that waved around his cheeks and down his neck. If I dig to the deepest corners of my memory, among the pocket-lint pieces of splintered sunlight and walnut crib bars against white apartment walls, I brush against an image of my pudgy baby body lying beside my brother on deep brown shag carpet, while above us my mustachioed father and his mustachioed brother faced one another with guitars, their corded arms strumming, faces lifted like wolves howling at the moon as their voices—for moments, mere fragments of breath—met in effortless harmony. I can't be sure if this is pure memory or something I created from stories my parents told me. My mom insists that Mac's spirit deposited this image in my mind on one of several nights in the mid-1980s when he haunted us, his restless spirit never satisfied that we were comfortable without him.

Mac called our apartment early on Labor Day morning in 1983, before the salty south Jersey air got humid enough to suffocate a person, to invite us all to spend the day at the swimming pool where he was a lifeguard. Bringing unbaptized Becky Jo to a public pool seemed like preparing a gift too tempting for the greedy hands of fate to ignore, so Daddy told Mac that we would meet him for a cookout later that night instead.

It was late afternoon when Mac finished his shift at the pool. His friends would tell us that he was setting up the chess set in his living room, heating the grill on the balcony, and only half paying attention when his buddy Davey arrived.

Davey had just bought a gun from a guy on a gambling run at Twosies Bar across the street. It wasn't anything fancy, a black snub-nosed .22 caliber revolver that fit in a jacket pocket, the sort of gun that wouldn't hurt too much to lose in a round of five-card stud. Davey strolled into Mac's apartment, put the gun to his temple, said, "Hey, look at this!" and pulled the trigger. Just joking, nothing to it, he hadn't loaded it anyway.

If you were the kind of person who measures the success of

a prank by its likelihood to cause heart attacks, this was a gold-medal winner.

The sun hadn't yet dropped below the horizon. My mom and daddy and we three babies were stuck in a traffic jam on the White Horse Pike when the next wave of guests walked in Mac's door. We couldn't have been more than fifteen minutes away when Mac picked up Davey's gun from the table, put it to his temple, and said, "Hey, look at this!"

There wasn't any blood, the story goes. Not like you see in movies. There was only a trickle that you could make out if you got close enough to check that Mac was breathing. Everyone in the apartment thought he was horsing around. It was a really great prank, until someone realized they needed to hide the drugs and call an ambulance. There was a bullet in the chamber that sheer idiotic luck had kept from nailing Davey when he'd demonstrated the same trick.

My mom and daddy pulled into the lot of the apartment building just as the EMTs were loading Mac's body in the ambulance. There was nothing that could be done but drive over to Grandmom Hall's house and tell her that her baby boy was gone. Better to hear news like that from family than from a police officer. Having a grandbaby to hug can soften such a blow, too, but baby Becky Jo was a screamy thing that sucked all the available comfort out of a room, making everyone's nerves raw and snappish. We didn't stay long.

After that Labor Day of 1983, my daddy started disappearing. For all we knew, he was mourning in his mother's basement, getting blasted with his construction buddies, or pawing into the ether for divine guidance to show him the way. He never packed a suitcase, never tipped his hand to us when he was planning an escape. He would go out the door one morning and not come back for days. Every time he left, it seemed like he would never return. On the nights when he did come home, he'd walk in the door, slip off his work boots, open a beer, and sit in the dark living room by himself. He'd be gone before breakfast the next morning and the cycle would start again.

With Daddy gone, Mom did something she hadn't done since she'd married him. She called her father in Oklahoma. The last time my mom had seen her father was when she was seventeen years old, the morning she ran away from his house in Oklahoma City. Reaching out after seven years of silence had to show my grandfather that my mother needed serious help. Mom called collect and Granddad accepted the charges. Then he sent his wife, my mom's stepmother, Mimi, to New Jersey to sort things out.

Mimi would say that she came because she had a more flexible schedule—Granddad worked for the Air Force, and Mimi was already retired—but she was also better suited to the task. My mom was alone with three kids under the age of three years old. The water and electric service had been shut off. Mimi was born during the Dust Bowl, and before she married my grandfather she'd raised a daughter on her own in 1950s Oklahoma. She'd seen enough low points in the human experience to be unemotional about things like cockroach trails among the mountains of dishes on the kitchen countertop, sweat-stained bedsheets, and three babies with full diapers. Mimi would tell me twenty years later that she had decided before she set foot on the plane to New Jersey that she was going to take one of us kids back to Oklahoma with her. Initially, she planned to take me. She said she'd never seen a milder baby.

Everyone in New Jersey told my mom that her third, screeching infant was her just dessert after Jacob and I had been so easy.

But Mimi sensed something wasn't right with my fussy baby sister. A trip to a pediatrician revealed that a muscle in Becky Jo's stomach had never fully developed. Everything she swallowed would come burning back up her throat and onto whoever was holding her at the time. Mom couldn't afford the medical care required to treat it. But Mimi and Granddad could.

So Mimi took Becky Jo back to Oklahoma. Temporarily. Until Mom could work things out with Daddy, until they could get back on their feet. I wonder if Mimi knew as she said those words—*just until you get back on your feet*—how unlikely that was to ever happen for my mom. I wonder if Mimi regretted not taking all three of us that day, or if she thought then that such a gesture would be an overcorrection, a permanent solution for a temporary situation, too devastating to our mother.

So because my daddy lost his brother, I lost a sister. There was a kind of logic to it that I never questioned.

But as soon as I was old enough to understand that I'd lost a little sister named Becky Jo, I understood that she was coming back to us someday. Mom uttered the phrase constantly *when Becky Jo comes home, when Becky Jo comes home.* When that day came I'd want to be able to catch her up on what she'd missed, to tell her the story of us, how we got split apart and how we came back together. I would collect facts, like the story of Uncle Mac, details like the aroma of hand-rolled cigarettes, sweat, and grease that announced the arrival of our father, or the way our mother's face was so white and her hair so dark that brushing the curls from her face in the morning was like uncovering buried bones.

It was my duty as an older sister to catalog these things. With each subsequent fracturing of our family tree, I would take a further step back from myself to get a better perspective, to see the whole picture, and preserve each image so I could share it later. If I stepped back far enough, if I focused on building my memory, I could become the narrator of our story as well as a character in it. That is how I came to see us, how I came to know myself and my family; from a distance.

A great loss can drive people apart or bring them closer together. For my parents, losing Becky Jo did the latter. Daddy started coming home regularly; he was less drunk more often. He picked up his guitar again and sometimes made it all the way through "Somewhere Over the Rainbow" while Mom put Jacob and me to bed.

Six months after Becky Jo left, my mom was pregnant again. She held off telling my daddy for months. Decades later, Mom told me about the night she delivered the news.

She waited until Jacob and I were asleep. The living room was dark. Daddy was sitting in his recliner, Mom wasn't even sure if his eyes were open. She said, *I'm pregnant.*

He said, *Okay.*

She said, *What do you want to do?* He didn't answer. I can imagine how the silence and the dark room and her husband with his eyes closed would have set her on edge. She said, *I don't want to name it if you're not going to be around; I don't want to keep it if you're not going to stay.* He said, *Okay.*

She asked if he thought he would want to be around. He said he'd have to think about it.

A month after Mom told him about the pregnancy, Daddy came home with a newspaper in his hand. He pointed out a classified ad from a couple looking to adopt. He said, *I think we should meet with them.* Mom said, *Fine.*

The phone number in the ad was for the other couple's lawyer, and it was in his office that they met the potential adoptive parents. Once Mom and Daddy were sitting across a wide walnut table from a pair of genuine adults who had college degrees, owned a house, had a lawyer, and desperately wanted a child, they seemed adolescent by comparison.

All at once, my mother knew what she wanted to do. Another world was suddenly available to this child, one with a two-car garage and a mother who wore sweater sets, a father with a good bank job. It seemed selfish to force this baby to share a one-bedroom apartment with two kids and two grown-ups, when she could have a house with a pool, a room of her own. So my mother decided she would give this baby up. But not to that first couple, not in that office that felt like it was judging her. My mother was going to do it on her own terms, on her turf. She would be the one asking the questions.

She called the lawyer the next day. She said she decided not to go with the couple they interviewed, but did he have anybody else? He said of course he did, and mom laid out her demands. She wanted to bring her kids with her this time, and the meeting would be on neutral territory. No offices or anybody's home. A coffee shop or shopping mall; someplace where they were all strangers. My mother was eight months pregnant by then; it was getting down to the wire when she packed Jacob and me into our winter coats on a January afternoon in 1985. She wanted to see how her daughter's potential new parents behaved around us, how they might treat a baby. If we liked these people, maybe everyone could feel good about the situation.

It was sixteen months after Becky Jo left us; I was two and half. All I knew of love was my mother's face and the way she let me boss her. *Wiggle your feet so I know you're awake, make me potatoes with things mixed inside. Tuck me in. Lemme pull your hair, scratch your back, wear your shoes. Look at me. Look at me. Look at me. Gimme some of what you have.* I could boss my brother, too. I loved him so much it excluded other people. When I first learned to talk, all I would say was Jacob for weeks and weeks. Then I learned to say, *Jacob, turn on the cartoons, reach me the cereal, boost me up on the countertop, bring me things, sing with me, STOP singing with me. STOP looking at me. Scoot over. Gimme some of what you have.* I got whatever I wanted because I was the littlest.

That day in 1985, I remember a long drive in Daddy's beige Oldsmobile. Mom, jittery in the front seat, kept saying, *We're late, we're late,* and that she hoped that *they don't think we changed our minds.* We left our coats on inside the car because the heater didn't work, and the wind came whistling through rusted-out holes in the sides. My daddy would flip this car a few months later. It wouldn't be the first time he fell asleep behind the wheel.

Outside the car window, naked trees swam together. If I kicked my legs as far as I could, my feet didn't touch the back of my daddy's seat in front of me. My brother must have looked how he always did in winter: his black hair tangled in his eyelashes and brushing against the collar of his puffy blue coat. He had one pointed ear; mom called it his fawn's ear. It poked out of his thatch of black hair like a pale mushroom on a forest floor.

Through the window there were birds. Lots of birds moving with a single mind like winged soldiers in formation.

Our journey ended in the parking lot of Olga's Diner next to Route 70 in Marlton. Our breath made clouds above our heads as my mom and daddy opened the car doors to grab Jacob and me for transport from car to building.

Inside the diner, another couple waited for us at a table. The other daddy wore eyeglasses. Their faces fishbowled as they leaned in to say, *What's your name?* to Jacob and me. I buried my

Please

head in the dark pocket between Mom's arm and her belly. I was not afraid, just quiet. After several minutes when no one paid attention to me, I turned around to peer through the ketchup bottles and iced tea glasses to see four pairs of grown-up hands on the table, knotting and unknotting themselves. Rings and watches knocked against plastic cups, metal forks, flaky wooden tabletop. My daddy's fingernails were ringed in black. He'd had to dig around the belly of the Oldsmobile to get her to start this afternoon, and his fingers were covered in grease. His fingers were always covered in grease.

I was sandwiched between my mom and daddy as the diner windows fogged over in the sunset. Jacob rat-holed himself under the spinny chairs at the long diner counter and Daddy had to collect him. From inside Mom's round belly, the heartbeat of my baby sister pulsed against my ear. The other parents must have known this was a test, that, if they passed, they would win a baby as their reward, the very baby girl that was resting in my mother's stomach just that minute.

I understood that this sister of mine was going to live somewhere else, away from us, like Becky Jo. This information did not make me think of the baby as less mine. She was my sister, like my brother was my brother and my mother was my mother. The adoptive parents' claim on my developing sister did not negate mine, she was not a kingdom or a territory or a thing with a deed; she was a person. This baby girl would be both my sister and these other people's daughter, and my mom's daughter. There would be moments when one claim took the focus—as right now this baby girl was more Ours than Theirs, and one day she would be more Theirs than Ours, but none of those connections could completely erase the others. It would be easier, perhaps, if they could, if after she was gone we could forget this baby ever belonged to us. But that's not how people work.

After the adults finished talking, my mom carried me through the diner and into the night air. Through the diner windows I could see the other mommy and daddy sitting in the booth. They didn't watch us go, but I watched them. They held hands on the table. They looked smaller and smaller as Mom made her way through the parking lot. She was warm and the air was cold and it was nice to have a nest of a person to snuggle in, but before I could get too comfortable we were back in the car, whistling down the road and back to our corner of the Garden State.

Daddy moved out the next day, packed his records and boots in boxes. We didn't see him for another month, until the day that Mom had the baby. She took a cab to the hospital alone, while a neighbor watched Jacob and me until our daddy could be fished out of whatever construction site he was on. He was still covered in sawdust and wet concrete when he picked us up.

At the hospital, he disappeared behind a set of double doors and Jacob and I were left in the white hallway. My brother was tall enough to look into a wide window above our heads.

"There are babies in there," he told me.

A woman came from behind the desk and lifted me up. Through the window was a room full of babies in clear cribs. The lady pointed to these red-faced bundles and told me, *This is a boy, that's a girl.* She pointed to one blue-eyed baby girl in the second row from the front.

"That's your sister," she said.

All the other babies' faces were squinched tight, looking like old men, but our sister had her eyes wide open, taking in the room around her. I waved at her in case she could see us. Her hands were wrapped tight against her tiny pink body; she couldn't wave back if she wanted to.

Our parents returned, Daddy pushing Mom in a wheelchair, and it was time to go. The lady put me back on the floor and I climbed into my mom's lap.

"Her name is Lisa," my mom said into my hair.

Marigold Court

After baby Lisa was adopted, my mom, Jacob, and I moved to another one-bedroom apartment. This was in Marigold Court, an apartment complex in the middle of Camden County, New Jersey. Camden County was like an apple; the bad spots oozed imperceptibly into the good ones. Our town was one of the not-so-bad spots in a county whose biggest bruise was an annual contender for "Murder Capital of the World."

Marigold Court was comprised of two brick buildings that faced one another across a cracked parking lot filled more with weeds than with cars. We were one of the 30 percent of families that the U.S. Census Bureau benevolently described as "female households with no husband present." Everybody in Marigold Court was.

It was 1986, the era of side ponytails and acid wash. On the radio Robert Palmer crooned about being addicted to love, while the Mothers of Marigold Court coped with the phantom limbs of absent husbands, boyfriends, and married lovers, while surrounded by tiny people—like me and my brother—who couldn't help that we were these men's miniatures.

The Mothers didn't have their own names, as far as I knew.

They were identified by the children they were attached to: Jimmy's-Mom, Manny-and-Monique's-Mom, Nick-and-Andy's-Mom, My-Mom. The Mothers had leathered tan skin, were thin enough that you could count their ribs, and had feathered hair that was short in the front and long in the back. They all wore the same outfit: in the summer, cut-off jean shorts, a striped tank top, and bare feet, and in the winter, Levi's and layers of long-sleeved shirts that their exes left behind. Except for My-Mom.

My-Mom's face was round and flat as a moon. Her brown hair fell in waves down to her shoulders and her wardrobe consisted exclusively of sweatpants and baggy tops. She was fair-skinned, golden-eyed, and sunburned like a newly shorn sheep if she stayed in the sun too long. She was petite, only five feet tall, but her breasts swelled with each of her pregnancies (four by 1986, but the Other Mothers didn't know that), which made her look a bit like a puff-chested pigeon.

I believed then that all families operated with moms and kids living in one place and daddies living somewhere else in a similar communal arrangement. The presence of a firehouse up the road from Marigold Court, housing a fraternity of firefighters, strengthened my theory. The firemen, in fact, made their way to Marigold Court with more regularity than any of our fathers did; they were the ones we called when a kid got his head caught in the balcony bars or climbed so high up a tree that he got stuck. The sight of the firemen was a jolt of testosterone that was worth every second when they came around.

The female residents of the complex appreciated the firemen's strong shoulders and finesse with a hatchet, but their admiration was less than sexual. They were relieved for the assistance of men no one had to sleep with in order to get something done. When the women did have the blessing of a fireman in their apartments, they usually asked him to reach that bowl that had been stuck behind the fridge for a year and to tighten the screws in her kids' bunk beds.

We always called them "firemen," but it seemed that when necessary they were paramedics, keepers of the peace, judges, priests, and notary publics. Firemen may have simply been the word the Mothers used for men they trusted to help without possible recriminations, a title for the men who ran in to help with the difficulties that had caused other men to run out. Asking for help was an act of bravery in Marigold Court. We all perched perilously on the knowledge that if the Mothers requested too much assistance from the wrong people—teachers, doctors, police officers, social workers, non-*firemen* people—us kids could be taken away. Taken away to where was never clear, but the idea of being removed from my mother was a fear that constantly pricked the back of my mind.

NONE OF the Mothers in Marigold Court were older than thirty-five, and all of their children were younger than fifteen. Our apartments didn't have phones, because the only people who wanted to contact the Mothers were bill collectors, former boyfriends, ex-husbands, or their parents (the ones who were still talking to them). There was no point in paying a phone bill if all your calls would be scoldings.

For emergencies, we used the pay phone at the end of the parking lot. The teenage girls milled around by that phone on the weekends wearing every belt they owned slung around their hips, fluffing their hair and smoking cigarettes while they waited for the phone to ring with an invitation to jump into some boy's car and drive someplace where they could use their fake IDs.

Some nights after everyone had gone to bed, I heard the pay phone ringing into the darkness. It was a faint chime that echoed around the parking lot. We were all asleep, or pretending to be. Whoever was on the other end of that line was someplace far away from here, and that ring, ring, ringing in the night was a reminder that, whether or not we could see it, there was a whole other world out there. A world that we were all better off not wanting, because it seemed not to care at all about us.

We kids spent most of our days tromping the plains of the lot between the facing buildings, communicating through grunts and howls. We didn't have many toys, but we didn't need them; the complex and its surroundings provided plenty of playthings. There was an overgrown field behind the apartment complex. No one knew whom the field belonged to, it was fenced in, but the gate was never locked. The packed earth path down the center of the field was the best shortcut to get to Mr. Ed's Corner Mart to stock up on Push Pops. This shortcut had been handed down from the older kids, and it was our job to tread it regularly to keep it clear for the ones who would come after us. It was the only heirloom we had, and this simple act made us part of something large, something important.

Wild grass grew on either side of the path, topping out at two feet above my head. Monique, a beautiful fourteen-year-old with braids running to the middle of her back and skin the color of diner coffee, told me that people let their dogs loose in the field after they turned mean and couldn't be around kids anymore; it was cheaper than having the dogs put down. Monique said that there were one hundred dogs in that field; a staggering number for which I had no frame of reference until she found a jar of pennies and we counted one hundred of them onto the sidewalk. Looking at all those pennies and imagining each one was a mean, lonely dog sent a shiver down my spine.

The set of railroad tracks that ran behind the buildings was the setting for Explorers, a game in which participants searched for things to place on the rails and be flattened when the train passed through. Whoever ended up with the most interesting flattened thing was the winner. There was Target Practice, in which we threw rocks at the dumpster at the end of the lot from farther and farther distances. When we tired of these games, we played Monster, in which the kid who had medically prescribed leg braces put them on and chased us. When he kicked you in the shins, you were out. It was like tag, but with more bruises.

The ground-floor apartments had giant sliding glass doors that opened onto the lot; it was as if the place were designed specifically for the convenient simultaneous viewing of *All My Children* and the antics of us little hooligans outside. The Mothers fluttered around Nick-and-Andy's-Mom's linoleum table like wasps around syrup, smoking Virginia Slims and waiting for welfare checks. Their earrings fluttered against nests of hair that barely moved, cocktail rings clicked against acrylic nails in a symphony of uniquely feminine composition. They wore drugstore perfume and sipped large clinking glasses of iced tea while they helped Jessica's-Mom paste together proofs of yellow-page ads. Jessica's-Mom got $1.50 under the table for each completed page she turned in to the phone book guy. The Mothers materialized in the parking lot when one of us hollered loud enough. All you had to do was scream, "Mom!" at the top of your lungs and whichever Mother drew the short straw came running.

I was a head shorter than any kids my age and bruised easily, so I spent most of my time sitting on the sidelines. My favorite retreat was the cool tile confines of the bathroom in our apartment. I laid flat on my back in the enameled bathtub and sang every song I could think of and some that I made up. The voice that vibrated through the iron tub and the surrounding tile seemed to come from outside of me and bounce back again; the low-level reverberation of the tub itself had a hypnotic effect. If we could pay the water bill that month, I would draw a bath and put my ears under the water to feel the voice stirring it like a sea breeze.

MANY OF the Mothers in Marigold Court were former foster kids, runaways, and high school dropouts; my mother was all of the above. My mother's parents were both from middle-class Philadelphia families. Her father, Charles, was an aircraft specialist for the Air Force. Her mother, Joan, was a homemaker. My mom, the youngest of three daughters, was born while Charles was stationed at the Royal Air Force Sculthorpe base in England.

In photographs from that time in the 1960s their family is catalog-perfect. Three little girls in white dresses tucked into a green lawn, smiling mother, handsome father. But Joan didn't like England. She wanted to go home to Philadelphia. She yearned for places she recognized, dinner with her sister, visits with her aunts. After my mother was born, Joan grew paranoid; started to see shadows everywhere she looked. Living in a city full of strangers didn't help assuage her anxiety. After my grandparents moved back to Philadelphia, Joan refused to move again. So Charles worked subsequent posts in New York and Mississippi alone, driving back to Philadelphia on long weekends to see his family. He wasn't exactly happy to do it, but he was willing to if it meant keeping the peace. He would have done it forever if Joan had been willing.

On the day Charles finished his assignment in Mississippi he came home to an empty house. He called around to Joan's friends until he located his wife; she was at a bar with her mother and had left the girls with her sister. Joan was less than thrilled to be dragged out of a bar by her husband. She fumed. She told my grandfather that she didn't love him anymore; she'd met someone else. She wanted a divorce. By the time Charles sent the papers— from his new post in Minneapolis—Joan could hardly remember asking for them. She stood in stocking feet in the front entry of their Philadelphia house and showed the fat envelop to her daughters. "He really did it," she said, over and over, first to them, then to herself. "He really did it."

It would be years before anyone realized that what really possessed Joan was paranoid schizophrenia. Her daughters knew something wasn't right, but they were little girls; no one paid any attention to their stories. When her husband was away, Joan had taken to hiding her children's shoes so they couldn't leave the house. She didn't send them to school, afraid that they would be turned against her. She was prone to rages. One day, at the end of a screaming argument with herself, Joan sent my mother away with the housekeeper. Just little Peggy, alone. All Joan's mental turmoil had started when Peggy was born, so surely the girl was the source of her problems. When social workers came to investigate, Joan told them that her husband had walked out on them. That she was overwhelmed. That it would just be temporary until she could get back on her feet. So my mom was placed in a foster home one town over from her sisters and her mother. She was six years old.

For months Mom asked her foster parents to call her father, he would come for her. *His name is Charles and he's in the Air Force*, she kept telling them, but they didn't look. They believed what Joan told them. And because Joan always managed to procure my mother for holiday gatherings and family functions, a year passed before Charles discovered that his daughter had become a ward of the state. By the time he found out, all the official paperwork said he had abandoned his family. Once it was part of the public record, how could he argue?

Peggy remained in foster care until she was twelve years old, when Social Services asked her were she wanted to live. She said, *I want to live with my dad.* Charles was remarried by then—to Mimi—and living in Oklahoma City. That reunification experiment lasted five years, in which time my mother failed out of ninth grade three times and then hopped a Greyhound bus back to New Jersey when she was seventeen years old. She ended up back in foster care when Joan called her a traitor and turned her away. That was when she met my daddy, Michael, in the summer of 1978, at a Christian summer camp. She was a camper, and he was a counselor. They prayed together around a campfire one night and were engaged three months later.

MY MOM, Jacob, and I had been living in Marigold Court for almost a year when I got the mumps and had to be quarantined. Mumps spread quickly in a group of kids, so I was sent away with Daddy.

"You can take care of her for one week," Mom told him when he knocked on our front door.

Daddy drove me to his mother's house and left me there. I lay on the gold brocade couch in my grandmother Hall's living room for three days. That is where I was when my mom met with the woman who would become my next little sister's mother.

Mom had become expert at hiding her pregnancies by now. She draped one of Daddy's old work shirts over her shoulders, and it hung straight down from her chest like a tent. She let people assume she was overweight; it was less embarrassing for people to think she was fat than to tell them she was still sleeping with her deadbeat husband. I didn't know she was pregnant until we went to the hospital again.

It was another girl, my third little sister. My mom named her Barbara, but the adoptive parents changed it to Rebekah. Never mind that we already had a Rebecca.

Once again, Daddy in his work boots wheeled Mom down the white hospital hallway while Jacob and I peered over the ledge of the nursery window looking for the clear crib with our name on it. No one picked me up to point out my sister this time, so I couldn't see her face. All I got was an eyeful of pink blanket pressed against the side of a crib that read HALL. In so many ways this new Rebekah was a repeat. A reprise. A variation on a theme; a record skipping.

When we added her to the litany of names at the end of our bedtime prayers, Jacob and I called her Rebekah Two.

Scars

In spring, a year after Rebekah Two's adoption, I was five years old. Jacob and I should have been in school but we overslept, so Mom brought us to the doctor's office with her.

The waiting room was warm and bright, full of round ladies and chairs big enough to accommodate them. A nurse called Mom's name and the three of us scurried through a door and down a hallway. Mom couldn't leave us in the waiting room because when we got bored Jacob and I started crawling under chairs and bothering people.

A nurse guided us into a cold room with a TV screen and Jacob and I sat in the one chair on the side while Mom stepped onto a table. She was as big as she had ever been.

The doctor dimmed the lights and said, "Let's see it," to my mom, who lay back on the table and lifted her baggy shirt above her waist. The doctor squeezed slime on the mound of my mom's belly. I sat up straight in the chair.

"It's okay, Meems." Meems was what she called me sometimes. "It's okay, he's not hurting Mommy," she assured me as the doctor smirked at me and rolled a stick with what looked like an eyeball on the end around in the slimy stuff.

The TV screen went black and then black-and-white. It was a cloud formation, a map of the ocean floor. I cocked my head to see. Jacob pinched me as my hair tickled his face.

"You're squashing me," he hissed.

I hopped out of the chair and onto the floor.

"There she is," the doctor said to my mom. "You want to see your little sister?" he said to me.

I nodded, and scooted up by my mom's head. She held my hand.

"Can you see it?" she asked me.

The doctor pointed to things on the screen. "This is her arm, she's on her side, see her nose there?"

The fuzz snapped into focus. I saw it. Saw her. That dark spot fluttering in the middle of the screen was her heart beating. I saw her.

The doctor said everything looked good. He printed out a sheet of pictures of the baby and put it in a thick envelope for Mom. Then we trotted out to catch the bus.

"We're meeting my friend for lunch," Mom said.

"Is Daddy going to be there?" Jacob asked, tucking his Tender-heart Care Bear in the corner of the seat so its plastic eyes could look out the window. My brother had taken to asking this question whenever we traveled anywhere.

"No," Mom said, "Daddy won't be there."

When we stepped off the bus, Jacob was in a deep sulk. He cried that he was *not hungry* and wanted to go *hooome*. Mom told him it wouldn't be long and he would get to eat french fries. The bus pulled away from the curb, its warm breath puffing against our ankles. We were two steps away from the bus stop when my brother gasped.

"My beaaaaar!" Jacob screamed. "We have to go back!"

Jacob looked down the street where the bus had lumbered away. We would never be able to catch it. I curled my hands into fists and rubbed my cheeks.

Mom knelt down on the sidewalk to be eye level with my brother. "I'm sorry," she said. Her eyes were soft with sincerity. She didn't try to make it better by offering a crappy grown-up assessment that it was just a bear and he could get another one. We couldn't always afford dinner; there certainly wasn't extra money lying around for new bears. Anyway, my brother didn't want a new bear; he wanted his bear.

Jacob's fawn's ear burned bright red as we walked up the street. He scuffed his feet along the sidewalk and twisted away from Mom and me. With the loss of the bear, the day had taken a turn. I was not hungry, either.

We walked half a block to a diner. Inside, a blond woman waved to us from a booth. Mom slid the photos from the doctor's office across the table to the woman. Her friend talked about getting ready for the Baby. When was the Baby due, what had the doctor said about the Baby?

I was hot and there were too many french fries on my plate. I hadn't noticed my mom's belly before, and now it felt like a lie somehow, that big belly hiding for so long under her baggy shirts. I was bored and tired of all the fuss and if I heard "the Baby" one more time I was going to dump my french fries all over the table.

We could never keep these little sisters, I had come to understand, because other people had more of everything. This blond woman owned a house in town and two on the shore. We didn't have enough room, enough clothes, enough food or laps to sit on or hands to hold.

The blond woman said they were thinking of names for the baby, Mark or Meghan or—

"It's a *girl*," I said into my plate of fries.

My mom and the other woman looked at me.

The woman smiled a warm smile that separated her from us.

A few minutes later, we were headed home on the bus. My brother walked the whole aisle and looked in every seat, but there was no Tenderheart Care Bear.

We stopped at the grocery store. I sat in the seat in the front of the grocery cart and Jacob spread out in the roomy bottom section. I worried over the picture of my little sister from the doctor's office, rolled it around in my mind with Becky Jo and Lisa and Rebekah Two while Mom examined the milk labels.

A grandmotherly woman brushed by our cart and waved at me.

"I have four baby sisters," I said to her.

"Isn't that nice," she said to me as she unfolded her grocery list.

"They don't live with us," I said.

The woman looked up from her list and over her shoulder, suddenly wondering who I belonged to. My mom put the milk in the cart with my brother.

"My Mary has a vivid imagination," my mom said as she pushed our cart around the corner.

On the short walk from the store to our apartment, my mom told me that we shouldn't tell anyone else about the baby girls.

"Why?" Jacob looked at the sidewalk in front of him.

"Other people don't . . . think like we do sometimes. They might not understand. If you want to talk about the baby girls, you can talk to me. But it's better if we don't talk to other people about them."

"Even Daddy?" Jacob said

Mom was quiet for a moment.

"Daddy is okay. You can talk to Daddy, too."

It was the first secret I had ever had; it felt luxurious to own something so important, but it also made me nervous. As soon as I had it in my possession, that secret tugged at me to be told.

I CAME close one early summer morning. Monique of the beautiful braids and coffee skin was coaching me how to walk like a TV lady. I was barefoot, wearing three of Monique's belts, and swishing through the overgrown grass in front of my apartment on the balls of my feet. I imagined that I was wearing high heels while Monique demonstrated a slithering sway step on the pavement. In her white denim jacket and bright miniskirt, she looked like a model on a catwalk. I'd managed a lower-back swivel dramatic enough to keep Monique's belts on my nonexistent hips (rather than slipping down my legs in a pile of vinyl like they had the first twenty-seven laps) and I sashayed right over a piece of broken window nestled like a land mine in the unmowed grass. My leg kicked up reflexively as pain shot up to my thigh. The glass was curved like a fishhook, cutting a jagged tear into the arch of my right foot. I hopped on my undamaged leg over to the curb to keep the glass from driving deeper into my flesh while Monique ran to dial the firemen.

As I sat alone on the curb, a thought overtook me as swiftly as the glass had cut into my flesh: A sister would be a nice thing to have in a time like this. A little sister might have been practicing a TV walk with me, might hold my hand when Monique left to dial the firemen, could marvel with me at how the glass in my foot caught the sunlight like a diamond.

The firemen arrived without sirens. The tall one located my mother while the freckled one bandaged my foot. Monique was beside me when the fireman said, "You're gonna have a nice scar, kid."

Monique sat close and said, "A scar! I got one, too." And she peeled up the sleeve of her white denim jacket to show me a dark raised spot on the inside of her left arm where her daddy had put out a cigarette when she was seven years old. And there it was: a pocket in the conversation that was the perfect size for my secret. It would have been easy. But suppose I told her and she looked at me like the lady had looked at my mom in the grocery store that day—startled, confused, fearful, judging? How would I feel then? Or suppose my mom found out that I told and was mad at me? I couldn't risk it.

The secret would build up a retaining wall against me and other people, cutting short the bonding moment that needed to happen in a friendship. No matter how close I got to people, I always held it back. But I would always know it was there, like the scar I now had on the sole of my right foot.

A few months later my next little sister was born. The name on the crib read HALL, but not for long, not forever.

Her adoptive mother named her Meghan, just like she said she would.

The Secondhand Washing Machine

The autumn when I began first grade, Daddy started making regular, daytime appearances in Marigold Court. I didn't know then—but would understand later—that my father had been paying late-night visits to our mother for a while, sleeping on the sofa in the living room while Jacob and I slumbered in the bedroom. Hence my long-lost sisters.

Daddy had replaced the beige Oldsmobile with a royal blue Ford Pinto whose rumbling purr could be heard half a block away. When we heard the car sputter into the parking lot in front of our apartment, Jacob and I ran for our coats and shoes because days with Daddy were full of adventures. He never made special plans when he took charge of us. He was going to treat us like grown-ups, he said. So he took Jacob and me on whatever activity he had previously arranged for himself. Jacob and I would dig around the backseat of the Pinto, piecing together two full seat belts if we could, and Daddy would tell us about Jesus, the Son of God, who was a carpenter just like him, as we drove through town delivering cash to the guys on Daddy's construction team. When he was invited to Christian ladies' houses to talk about the Bible, Jacob and I sat at his feet, listening to them argue about whether the devil had one goat foot and one chicken foot or two hoofed feet. That I had nightmares about a chicken-footed devil watching me sleep for months afterward was a small price to pay for my introduction into such a magical new world.

The best nights were when Daddy had a deejay job. Those times I would wear a dress and dance behind the deejay booth while older people in nice shoes bribed me with sugary drinks to bring their song requests back to my daddy and heckle him until he played them. *Daddy, play "Hot Hot Hot"!* I would say, bouncing from one socked foot to the other, my face slick with sweat. *Play Madonna, play Michael Jackson, play "La Bamba."* My hair would spring loose from my ponytail and curl around my face like whiskers.

Most often, though, he took us to jam sessions. These were always held in a house on the edge of town with no neighbors close enough to complain about noise. Light burned through cracks around the window frames and into the night. Daddy pulled his guitar from the trunk of the Pinto and we walked without knocking straight into the living room, where a rotating cast of six to ten other men gathered around instruments of various shapes and sizes. Guitars, bongo drums, fiddles, mandolins; the only instrument that never made an appearance was a piano. Someone pulled out a pitch pipe and blew a clean E4 and the living room filled with the wandering hum of fiddles and guitars trying to match that pitch. When the unique voices of each instrument met one another on the same note, the satisfaction filled my belly with a warm belief in the goodness of the world.

Soon the men lit musky-sweet-smelling pipes and sent us kids down to the basement. But I usually sat at the top of the stairs to listen. The other men in the room worried over their instruments with pencils behind their ears, stopping every few minutes to curse and scribble notes. But my daddy played his guitar like most people hold a fork; it was an extension of his arm and did whatever he willed it to. His silky baritone voice blended with whatever anyone was singing, but was strong and clear when the other men forgot the lyrics and he had to forge ahead alone. Leaning off the edge of a sofa, tapping his feet on the floor, and singing sad songs about dry levees, my daddy was lit up from the inside. Everyone within arm's reach wanted to bask in the glow he gave off.

After a couple of hours, the other men's fingers were too tired to play. That was when Daddy started talking about Jesus and Salvation, which must have been his plan all along. This was his ministry. My father had always wanted to be a missionary, an honest-to-God traveling baptizer and house builder. When marriage, children, and lack of funds kept him from going to Africa to preach the gospel, it seemed he sought out the low-hanging fruit here in South Jersey. These jam session guys were to my daddy what prostitutes and tax collectors were for Jesus: souls to be saved.

The guys didn't have much good in their lives—wives left 'em, factory work dried up—and the only comfort they could dependably lay hands on was a six-pack of Coors and a worn Fender guitar. Zoned out on music, weed, and booze, these guys didn't stand a chance against the stone-cold charisma of my daddy when he got fired up on Jesus.

"Let the Lord and Savior into your heart, man," he'd say, clapping a firm hand on some sad guy's shoulder. "He will transform you. Give Him the power."

Everyone wanted to feel savable when he talked that way. I wondered about the mechanics of it when I heard my daddy say

Let the Lord and Savior into your heart. Was there a door inside me that was waiting to be opened? I wondered how Jesus could be in my heart, and Daddy's, and the hearts of all these men at the same time, and figured it had to be some arrangement like the one Santa Claus had with all those guys in red suits at malls.

ONE NIGHT Daddy saw me sitting at the top of the basement stairs and said, *Come over here, Pumpkin, let me introduce you,* and I scrambled to his side. He lifted me onto the coffee table among the beer bottles and cigarette papers and said, *You men should hear my baby girl sing.* I wasn't expecting to be put on the spot like that, but I had learned "This Little Light of Mine" at a Vacation Bible School, so I belted it out.

Years later, when I was buried in religion myself, I would learn that singing was a form of meditation that—when strategically placed in a religious service—let the sinners think on the sermon they'd just heard and see how they could stitch it into their lives. My father had discovered this magical quality without a single day in a seminary.

I tried to make my voice fill the corners of the room. I could see a sense of calm wash over the glassy, bloodshot eyes of the men as the words of my daddy's sermon ping-ponged around in their smoky heads. I was part of Daddy's act now; I was the ringer.

When I finished singing, the men clapped and I curtsied. It was a move that I stole from a Shirley Temple movie and practiced with Monique until I got it right; I was jazzed that I had a place to use it. But when the applause ended, Daddy left me standing on the coffee table for a moment too long. I felt a wind blow through the cracked windows.

The boozed-up men started slurring, *Dawlin', come on, gimme a kiss*. It was a slippery troublesome sound; pawing at me to give them a thing that wouldn't ever fill the bottomless pit of dislike those poor drunk men had for themselves. Their scratchy faces were filled with a hungry lonesomeness so deep that looking into their eyes was like gazing down a well. The Christian thing to do was go on and kiss their sad, grizzled cheeks—which I guess was why my daddy didn't tell them to knock it off—but I didn't want to. I was a self-preserving kid, and as soon as one of those rough-handed musicians lifted me off the coffee table I ran down to the basement like the devil was chasing me with chicken-claw feet.

To cap off that strange night, the Pinto refused to start when we wanted to leave. This was not unusual; after it had time to nestle into a parking space, we always had to sweet-talk it and give it a few minutes. I kept digging in the backseat for the seat belt while Daddy went from the normal coaxing—*Come on . . . you can do it . . . come on, girl*—to the kind of swearing he did when kids were around—*Shoot! Son of a . . . son of a . . . gun. God . . . darned Pinto.* Once my daddy started son-of-a-gunning, he was close to the scarier, angrier place where he would bark at us to *stop crying or I'll give you something to cry about* and swing his arms around until he broke a window. This time he stopped short of those histrionics.

"We'll have to walk to the bus stop," he finally said.

The bus stop was a mile and a half away. We were in the middle of nowhere, there weren't even sidewalks for most of our trek. There was nothing but trees, high grass, and icy wind blowing off the Delaware River. Compared to Marigold Court, this was wilderness.

"Look how many stars you can see without all the city lights in the way!" Daddy crowed. He was pointing out the Big Dipper when it started to rain. It was just a spitting rain at first, but by the time we reached a sidewalk, it had turned to a downpour. The rain soaked us as it fell from the sky, then bounced off the pavement to hit us again. My feet squished in my shoes. Daddy promised that *one day we'll look back at this and laugh*, but I couldn't see how.

So when I heard the Pinto sigh into the parking lot on a late October evening, I prepared to hide in the closet. I didn't want to face another night of sad men and rainy walks. It was Mom's birthday. Monique had come over to watch Jacob and me while my mom feathered her hair and shimmied into a black-and-pink-striped sweater dress, and then Stevie's-Mom took her out for a drink at the bar down the street. She'd been gone for half an hour by the time the Pinto arrived, accompanied by the deeper rumble of a pickup truck. Jacob ran to open the curtains.

Daddy tapped on the glass and Monique hollered to him that she was not supposed to let anybody in. Daddy pointed to a washing machine in the bed of the pickup truck. *I'm just here to deliver a present*, he said. Monique opened the door, and soon he had sweet-talked her into helping him get the other Mothers in the building to join us for a surprise party. He pulled beers from the trunk of the Pinto and chilled them in the fridge. He ordered pizza while Monique ran around the complex knocking on doors. A paunchy man climbed out of the pickup truck and helped my father wrestle the washing machine into the apartment.

It was mustard-yellow and wheeled, so you could roll it out of a closet and attach it to the kitchen sink to fill with water. The dings and floppy dials suggested that it had already lived a long life. I couldn't imagine ever wanting a secondhand washing

machine for my birthday, but maybe Daddy knew something I
didn't.

Soon other Mothers started arriving in groups of two and
three to obscure the fact that they had rendezvoused over vodka
and Cokes in Nicole's-Mom's living room and dished the good
dirt about this birthday business before they arrived at our place.
The crumbs of the conversation they had started there slipped
out under their breath as they milled around our apartment.
This *Johnny-come-friggin'-lately,* they've *got his number,* they've *seen
Hail Mary passes like this before.* Before we had plowed through all
the pizzas, my father ordered everyone into the kitchen and we
scrambled around the washing machine.

The steel was cold against my cheek and the Mothers' legs
were warm behind me. When Daddy turned out the lights, it was
like the apartment had closed its eyes with us inside. I couldn't
see my *hand* right in front of my *face.* Shushes buffeted me like
waves.

The front door jiggled and we all held our breath. Feathered
bangs rustling behind me sounded like a nest of beetles rubbing
their legs together. My mom stumbled through the door.

"It'sh just like him to comp*lete*ly forget my birthday."

"Hey, Peggy, were all these lights off when we left?" Stevie's-
Mom said, trying to give my poor drunk mom a hint.

"Wait! I got some Ding Dongs in my purse, we'll put a candle
in that. Happy friggin' birthday, *Peggy* . . ."

Her keys jingled as she crossed the living room. When she
hit the kitchen, her feet slid slushily across the linoleum. She was
only a foot away from us, but hadn't looked up. She flipped on the
lights. We all yelled, "Surprise!"

Daddy hugged her, and gestured to the washing machine

like a model on *The Price Is Right*. Hadn't Peggy, just last month, informed him that doing laundry required her to load a double stroller with me on one end and a trash bag full of dirty clothes on the other, strap a backpack of laundry detergent on Jacob, and walk three full blocks to the Laundromat? Hadn't she insisted then that he help out more?

See, he *did* listen.

Once the Mothers realized there was nothing to see after the big reveal, they snapped up the last slices of pizza and headed back to their own apartments, humming about *surprise party my ass,* and *bet that hunk of metal doesn't even work.* It was hours past my bedtime and I fell asleep under the kitchen table.

I woke up when Daddy moved me from the floor to my bed. Mom was behind him saying, "You know that's not what I meant." She didn't look mad; she was smiling in a funny way.

Daddy told her in a low grumbling voice about a fiftieth wedding anniversary he'd deejayed a few months ago, how beautiful it was. How it made him think that if that couple could make it through one world war, three heart attacks, and a recession, maybe my parents could figure out how to navigate the tail end of the 1980s. He kissed Mom on the forehead as he squatted to place me on my bed. Mom said, "We'll see."

A couple days after the surprise party, I was standing on a kitchen chair watching the wash spin in the mustard-yellow machine when Daddy dropped in again. He said he wanted to show us something and herded my mom, Jacob, and me into the Pinto. We drove across town and into the city of Camden, stopping behind a brick town house. We entered through the back door, into a narrow cream-colored kitchen, and Daddy started to show us our future. "The table would go here," he said. "The living room is this way . . ." This place had stairs, separate floors, a basement where he could hook the washing machine into the main lines so we wouldn't have to roll it around the kitchen.

"There's room to bring back Becky Jo," Mom whispered.

"That's what I was thinking," Daddy said.

There were two bedrooms and yards in the back and front, space to put the things I saw in commercials: plastic pools, Slip 'N Slides, games with nets.

"What do you think?" Daddy flipped his keys in this hand.

Mom tapped her fingers on the plaid contact-papered kitchen countertop. She looked at me and Jacob running around the room where the table would go. She said, "Okay."

We moved out of Marigold Court the next day. The Mothers stood outside Nick-and-Andy's-Mom's apartment smoking cigarettes and crossing their arms. To the women we left behind, we would become the story of the Mother whose deadbeat husband bought her a secondhand washing machine, the Mother who packed up her children, left the crumbling confines of Marigold Court, and lived happily ever after in a town house on the other side of the railroad tracks.

I looked out the wide back window of the Pinto as we pulled out of the parking lot. The Mothers stamped out their cigarettes and went inside, back to the linoleum table. In the days to come, I imagined their crackling voices passing our saga between them when they got tired of sad stories and were ready for a hopeful one.

Because Lord knows if it could happen to us, it could happen to anybody.

Bringing Becky Back

The new house had two bedrooms and two floors, three if you counted the basement (which I didn't because it was dark and smelled like old socks). Double cellar doors led from the basement to the backyard. In the summertime, a person could situate a plastic pool at the base of these doors, loop the garden hose around the door handle, and have a decent waterslide. Some water would leak into the basement from this arrangement, but nobody worried about that; it wasn't like we owned the place.

Our furniture consisted entirely of cast-offs from friends and family members. We didn't have much of it and none of it matched. Everything we owned would have been left on the curb for garbage pickup if our apartment weren't available as the last way station before the dump. Our television sat on top of an elaborate old stereo table with a broken record player built in. There was a dusty brown recliner and a once-gold-embroidered sofa from Daddy's mother's house. The kitchen had no room for any furniture outside of the built-in cabinets, and the dining room had just enough space to fit a gray glass-top table and a few furry brown chairs whose headrests fell off daily, exposing the pointed ends of the screws beneath.

Jacob and I shared a bedroom, and Mom and Daddy had a separate one. Jacob's and my room had space for both of our twin beds pressed against opposite walls and a strip of carpet down the center. Two windows opened onto the sagging roof of the front porch, which Mom told us we were never to play on. Stray cats sunned on our front porch and sheltered their kittens in our basement.

My parents were serious about bringing Becky Jo back, but first they needed the money for airfare. Mom went back to cashiering at a department store and added the graveyard shift at a fast-food restaurant five nights a week. Daddy continued with construction during the day and deejay jobs at night. They passed my brother and me between them like footballs. During times when their work schedules overlapped they left us under the care of a neighborhood teenager who didn't mind being paid next to nothing.

The neighborhood was a strip of flat-faced two-story buildings rubbing up against each other. It had been built as a federally planned housing development in the early 1900s, a place for a nearby shipyard to house the men who built boats for World War I. Hallways were tight, ceilings were low. The street crowded quickly at dusk when the workingmen came home, but that didn't stop us kids from playing touch football right in the middle of the road, daring them to run us over.

Our apartment was in a triplex that curved around a shared front lawn. We lived in the middle unit. On our right was a family of Indian immigrants with two children; Donna, who was fourteen years old, and Sal, who was eight. Sal was a bony little kid with a terrier complex—he didn't think that any adventure was too big for him. Sal, Jacob, and I became a trio immediately. He was new here, too, and we took to exploring the neighborhood together. Our neighbor on the other side of the triplex was an old man named Albert who either couldn't afford dentures or refused to wear them. I never understood a word he said. He was always yelling, which contributed both to my difficulty deciphering his words and his frustration at not being understood.

There were more daddies in this neighborhood than we had encountered in Marigold Court. Most of the daddies worked construction, on a factory line, or as mechanics. The mothers here had the threat of, "Just wait until your father gets home," which added a new dimension to punishment. Unlike the empty swats of someone's mom, daddies could do serious damage. Give them a couple of beers after a long day and they started growling and scratching around for something to hit. In the absence of a good fight or a wayward child, the daddies punched out walls. It seemed to me that everybody who had a daddy had a hole in their house somewhere.

In June 1989, Jacob and I were left alone with our daddy for a week when Mom went to Oklahoma to bring our sister Becky Jo back home. It was a month before my seventh birthday, which made it a month before Becky Jo's sixth birthday. *Irish twins*, Daddy called us.

I'd met my sister, briefly, when I was five years old, when Mimi and Granddad had driven cross-country to take her to Disney World. We met up with them for dinner at a Chinese restaurant. My memory of that visit was marred considerably by my bitterness at not being invited to accompany them to the Magic Kingdom. But I was prepared to forgive my sister for meeting Mickey Mouse without me. She was coming back and nothing that had happened in the past would matter.

The day that Mom and Becky Jo were scheduled to return, I put on my Easter dress and hat and gloves to meet them. It was my special-occasion outfit, and if anything was a special occasion, this was it. We were going to be a real family now, our baby sister was coming home to us because we had been very good; everything was going to be rainbows and fried chicken dinners from now on. I could feel it. Our family would be, if not complete, at least a big step closer.

After shoving enough toys under the beds and into the closet so a vacuum could be run in our bedroom, Jacob and I sat on the couch in the freshly scrubbed house trying not to run into the kitchen and bust into the ice-cream cake we both knew was in the freezer. Each moment that passed was a breath closer to the inevitable second when one of us would spill or break something. Daddy rooted around in the basement and procured a roll of butcher paper along with the wormy ends of a can of house paint that he'd liberated from a job site, with which Jacob and I painted a sign that read WELCOME HOME, BECKY JO! with a smiley face. We managed, miraculously, not to get paint on anything but the paper, but we got overeager and hung the sign before the paint had dried all the way. The smiley face dripped into a sloppy cloud. It didn't matter. I was thrilled to have a sister, someone lower than me in the pecking order. She would be equal parts my comrade and my minion.

But when my sister and Mom walked in the door and saw the sign, Becky Jo said, "My *name* is Rebecca."

I looked at her. Her storklike legs poked out of baby-blue short-shorts; she had blond streaks in her straight, straight hair, and blue eyes. She was taller than me by at least two inches.

I'd never cared if anyone liked us before. Other people's ideas about our family never mattered. But now, under the inquisitive gaze of someone—my sister—whom I wanted desperately to like us, our scraggliness and weirdness took on dimension and gravity. Those words—"My *name* is Rebecca"—landed like a brick to my head. They were an affirmation that she did not want to belong here. Here, where suddenly everything was bathed in the kerosene smell of fresh Raid, the places where the cats had built their own exits in the window screens gaped like empty eye sockets, my knees were scuffed beneath my Easter dress, and the welcome sign we'd painted looked like house paint splattered on butcher paper. Which it was; I had just hoped that our love and affection would transform it into a masterpiece.

I ran forward to hug her. I took her by the hand and ran her around the house to show her where we made room for her. I opened the drawers in the big white bureau that I'd emptied just for her. I showed her Jacob's bed by the bedroom door, and the double bed that she and I would share by the window. I thought that by showing her all the effort we'd put in to conjure her, maybe she'd give us partial credit. Here was where we had saved a place for her; here was where she fit. She might think she didn't know us, but I felt that I knew her intrinsically: I knew what her blank expression meant because I made the same one. I saw how she was pulling her eyelids wide open because blinking would make her cry. I held her hand. I grabbed it whether she wanted me to or not. We were linked. I could feel it, though it was hard to see just yet.

In our shared bed that night I rolled over to whisper in Rebecca's ear all the things that she'd missed. I told her how Uncle Mac was supposed to be her godfather but then he shot himself in the head, and then Mom and Daddy had a baby that they gave away, then another one, and another one, all girls. I told her that the sisters were a secret, that they were *our* secret, that Rebecca was one of us now, that she always had been but now she was here, and—

"My godfather is Granddad's nephew," she said.

I kicked free of the covers and pulled my right foot up to my chest, confused.

"Look," I said. "I got this scar when I stepped on a piece of glass."

Rebecca was quiet. I showed her the smooth hairless spot on my right forearm.

"This is where I got burned when the living room lamp fell on me," I told her.

Still nothing.

"You can show me your scars if you want to," I prompted her.

"I don't have any," she said.

My sister was as exotic as the snow leopard at the Philly Zoo: shiny, well fed, and obviously grown in different soil than the rest of the kids in our neighborhood. The Becky Jo that I had built in my head over the past six years was my double. She wore dresses, threw tea parties, and would let me braid her hair. But *Rebecca* wore pants, and got muddy and grass-stained when she ran. She didn't like eating cold hot dogs from the fridge, and she didn't want to model all her dresses for me. When we opened each subsequent box that arrived from Oklahoma, she hollered as I touched our new toys, "That's *mine!*" Over six years, Rebecca had grown accustomed to being an only child. She had been "spoiled," all the adults said. Spoiled; for what, I could not immediately discern, but cursory investigation revealed that she didn't know simple things like the rules to kick-the-can, or how to cut her own meat. Only when she got hurt would she start looking for someone to snuggle up to.

Being without adult supervision in the free fall of afternoons in the neighborhood before the parents arrived home was a particular challenge. In Oklahoma, Rebecca had spent her days surrounded by grown-ups. Our neighborhood teemed with children. With one to four kids in every apartment for blocks and blocks, we handily outnumbered the adults, who frequently left us to fend for ourselves when they went to work or to drop off rent checks. The place was more ours than theirs, it seemed. It was a difficult transition for my sister.

On the day we climbed up to the roof of the school garage with Jacob and Sal, Rebecca froze. "I can't get down," she said. Her face had gone pale and her knees wobbled.

"Just jump," I said.

My sister shook her head. Jacob and Sal were already down on the ground, calling up for us to jump already, it was only six feet, right into freshly mowed grass. But Rebecca didn't move.

"I'll get Mom, okay?" I said. "Would you like that?"

Rebecca nodded. I shinnied down the rainspout and raced to the apartment, where my mom was folding laundry.

Mom stood by the rainspout and said, "All you have to do is come halfway. I'll bring you the rest; I'm right here."

My sister slid down the drainpipe, cautiously, into Mom's arms.

Rebecca was far too big to be carried, but she wouldn't release her grip on Mom's shoulders. Her feet slapped against Mom's knees for the three blocks home.

But maybe I shouldn't have done that. It didn't teach my sister anything; Rebecca continued to look for adults to entertain her, state rules, and dole out punishments. Like the day we got tangled up with the Secretary.

About a week after Rebecca came home, a Secretary and her handyman husband moved into the house on the corner. They were a new breed of tenant for our block. Most every household in a mile radius harbored litters of children fed by free school lunches, or retired Social Security recipients. These two fresh faces were doughy, hopeful. Not like us. They arrived childless and ready to polish up the crumbling brownstone they'd purchased. Otherwise, they seemed to ignore everyone around them. They didn't sit on their front porch and holler at the neighbors over cans of Coors, or leave their front door open behind the screen door like everyone else. They went in their back door, and stayed inside hammering and refinishing until one of them had to leave for work again. Every few days or so, I would see the Secretary watching our neighborhood game of street football from the safety of her front window, her form slim and shadowy behind her lace curtains. One rare day, the Secretary ventured from her brownstone in the early afternoon, dragging a refrigerator box to the curb.

The box looked about the size of a pop-up playhouse I'd seen at the Bonanza Supermarket a week before. It was available for "10 cereal box tops and $5.95 shipping." The length of time required to accumulate so many box tops—not to mention the $5.95— seemed interminable, so when I first laid eyes on that refrigerator box, I considered it a gift.

I scrambled inside the box, to claim it before another neighbor kid could snap it up. Its cardboard confines were quiet and cool, until Sal tumbled in after me (with much less stealth). We were figuring out where to cut the first window when the storm struck. The Secretary began shaking the box and yelling for us to "get out of there this *instant*."

I thought if we were quiet, maybe she would go away, but she rattled that box like we were the last two Raisinets stuck to the bottom.

"Boxes are dangerous to play in," she roared as Sal and I rolled out into the daylight.

"You step on a staple, you'll get tetanus, and your arms and legs will fall off," she said as we skittered back to the shelter of my front porch.

Considering the parking lots and abandoned sheds that were our usual playgrounds, staples seemed like a silly thing to worry about. Plus, we had to be inoculated against pretty much everything in order to qualify for free milk and school lunches. The Secretary either didn't know this or didn't care, and proceeded to slash my new playhouse to pieces with a razor blade while Sal and I watched.

From the length of our front yard, the Secretary looked so thin that a stiff breeze could blow her over. Up close, she towered over us with her dark eyes firing and her face twisted into shades of concern, condescension, and pity. She seemed to simultaneously like and loathe being the only responsible person on our block, but that was what she got for moving to this neighborhood for the cheap real estate.

It was a summer Saturday. The day was a warm bath, not unpleasant, but stagnant. The government-funded "recreation" program at the public school—designed to dissuade us from reckless shenanigans while our parents were working—was not running. We were home all day under the clumsy supervision of Sal's sister, Donna. Though Donna was fourteen, she was barely taller than me.

Sal and I were mourning our loss by stomping down anthills in the front yard when Rebecca's wail chain-sawed the early afternoon quiet. She shot out of our house and into the amphitheater of the lawn we shared with our neighbors. Rebecca had played too rough with a kitten, and this time the kitten had lashed back, scratching her near her left eye. Jacob and Donna came running out after Rebecca, and all five of us—Rebecca, Donna, Sal, Jacob, and me—were standing in the front lawn when the Secretary took interest in our drama.

The Secretary stalked out of her house—faster than I thought she could—right onto our turf. Khaki-shorted and red-cheeked, she sneered at Donna. "Babysitter? You can't be more than ten years old yourself." She took my sister's face in her hands and asked, "Where are your parents?"

My brother's face was blotchy and red as he delivered the answer that had been drilled into us for years:

"They're working and they'll be home soon."

While this line usually worked on Jehovah's Witnesses, landlords, and gas meter-readers, the Secretary was unsatisfied. She told Sal and Donna to go home, that she'd take care of *this*, as she dragged our little sister into her house. It all happened so fast.

When Rebecca slinked back to our house, Jacob and I were sweating in the living room with the curtains closed and all the doors locked. Our sister was embarrassed, and she should have been. The ointment shining on the corner of her disinfected eye was a mark of disloyalty, making her different from Jacob and me. But we all three had broken an oft-spoken rule: we'd talked to a Stranger.

The only sound in the room was the three of us blinking, and my heels thumping the cushions of the brown chair in the corner while we waited for our heart rates to slow back to normal. Then there was a knock.

Jacob was the man of the house, so he looked out the window and opened the door. I was sure it was the cops coming to take us away for talking to a stranger; for letting our little sister go into a stranger's house *on our watch*. After a few whispered exchanges, Jacob closed the door, holding a basket of sandwiches.

"She made us lunch."

He placed the basket in the middle of the floor and we pondered its unlikely presence in our living room. I was sure it was poison.

Why should we trust her? No other adult had ever dropped by the house with a suspicious basket of sandwiches when our parents weren't home. This was exactly how the snake convinced Eve to eat that apple in the Bible, and how evil queens dispatched with inconvenient princesses in all kinds of fairy tales. Jacob unwrapped one foil packet as though he were handling a live grenade.

It was brown bread with the crusts on.

Tuna fish. With pickles chopped up inside.

Poison, clearly. In an act of silent solidarity, we threw the sandwiches into the jungle grass of the backyard, where the cats promptly gobbled them up. If the cats dropped dead, then I couldn't have any sympathy for them. They were just cats, after all, and in this neighborhood, cats were as ubiquitous as cockroaches and cars on cinder blocks.

Those sandwiches reminded us that we were hungry, so we rolled bologna and American cheese into torpedoes that we slurped down with red Kool-Aid. We sat in the middle of the living room floor, staring at each other and trying not to talk about what was going to happen when our parents got home from work.

In the back of all of our minds we knew we'd betrayed them. We knew they were doing the best they could with only one high school diploma between them. Just because it was summer didn't mean that our parents could take time off of work to keep an eye on us twenty-four hours a day. Work was the glue that kept this little life together. Pretty soon it'd be September, when we'd all need corduroys and new shoes to start school. And if the Camden County Department of Education wasn't able to keep an eye on us, our parents would have to find a babysitter they could afford. All we had to do to was keep a lid on it; not be so bananas that we drew any attention. Mom would only be gone for five hours! Couldn't we keep it together for five hours? Apparently, we could not.

Our mother got home first. We were terrible liars, so Jacob told the whole story. He pointed out where we had thrown the sandwiches in the backyard. Mom's face became wolfish; her eyes narrowed, her jaw set. I had never seen this face before. She was primitive, grotesque, galvanized.

"Where is she?" Mom said.

Jacob cracked the front door with trepidation. I slipped behind it and watched through the gap in the doorframe as Jacob led the way to the Secretary's house. Every blade of grass they brushed through sharpened. My mother grew a foot taller as she crossed the yard.

Mom told the Secretary to keep her nose out of other people's lives. Mom told her that she had no business sending our babysitter home. The Secretary told Mom that if she saw us running around "like feral children" again, duty required her to call the Department of Children and Families.

Mom understood, of course. She was sorry, she said. She was sorry that the Secretary was a barren bitch who didn't have any children of her own, but she'd better stay away from us, or duty would require Mom to call the cops. And just so she didn't get any funny ideas about whose side anybody was on, the Secretary should know that Peggy's kids fed those fucking sandwiches to the cats.

Rebecca started taking note of how we operated after that. When some kid locked me in a suitcase a few days later, Rebecca ran and got Jacob, rather than the nearest grown-up. Together my brother and sister tackled the kid and left him with a black eye. Soon she was jumping off garage roofs and eating slices of American cheese out of their plastic sleeves just like the rest of us.

By the end of her first month with us, Rebecca was no longer surprised by meanness or danger; she expected it. And when the time came for her to take her licks—as it did the day that an older girl punched her in the stomach without any reason except that Rebecca was new—my sister set her jaw and she didn't cry.

Leaving Jersey

Since Rebecca's arrival, Mom made a point to spend time with each of us individually. It was more economical than trying to do something as a group of five, and it was nice to have a few hours alone with my mom even if my turn only came around once a month.

Which meant that a week before I started second grade, Mom took me to get my ears pierced at the Piercing Pagoda at the mall where she'd worked during the holiday season. I decided on a pair of silver studs shaped like teddy bears and the woman behind the counter loaded them in a pink gun. She looked me in the eyes and asked, "You want your mom to hold your hand?"

I shook my head no; I was resolved about this piercing business. I was eager to work my way up to wearing shoulder-grazing hoops and clanging feathery affairs like the teenage girls in the neighborhood.

The gun clicked loudly in each of my ears; it didn't even sting.

With my new, bear-shaped studs in my lobes, Mom and I headed on home. She kept saying, "Don't play with 'em or they'll get infected," but I couldn't keep my fingers from turning the studs just a little bit.

As we rounded the corner from the bus stop onto our street, we saw Jacob and Rebecca sitting on the front porch roof that we were never supposed to sit on. They had their legs dangling over the edge, watching the sunset. Mom started to run, yelling, "What are you doing up there?"

"Their dad said they could," Donna said from her porch next door, where she was trimming the ends of her hair with a pair of kitchen shears.

In thirty seconds flat, Mom was in the front door and up the stairs. She opened the windows in our bedroom and pulled my siblings inside as she puffed, "What if you fell? What if you'd have died? What would I do then?"

Jacob and Rebecca didn't protest or apologize. Mom didn't seem to notice, but I was puzzled. Something was up with them, but I couldn't tell yet what it was.

Daddy was in the alley behind the apartment, sorting through boxes of records in the trunk of the dead Pinto. Mom yelled at him that children should not be allowed to sit, unsupervised on an ancient porch roof that holds on to rainwater so good that it might as well be a reservoir.

"Donna was right there," Daddy said grandly, keeping his voice mellow for the benefit of the gathering neighbors.

Mom snarled, "Yes, because their father was playing in the backyard."

A truck pulled into the alley behind the apartment and honked twice; it was one of Daddy's disc jockey buddies. They were splitting a wedding gig tonight.

"They're fine. Everybody's fine. I gotta go," Daddy said, maintaining the calm and unbothered tone that made Mom clench her fists so hard that her knuckles popped.

Daddy heaved a milk crate full of records out of the Pinto's trunk and into the bed of the truck. Then he was gone.

Mom retreated to her bedroom. I could hear her opening drawers and dumping out boxes from the closet; she was looking for something. Amid the clatter, her breath was jagged and audible. She'd been breathing funny all day, but it'd gotten louder and wheezier since we got home. When I heard the rummaging stop in her bedroom, I went to check on her. I found her sitting on the side of her bed, holding a piece of foil that had been folded into an elaborate pipe, like ones I used to see at jam sessions with Daddy. The room was a war zone; clothes and shoes covered the floor and the bed. The rolled-up shades were askew and the twilight glow coming through them cast everything in a chilly blue-gray. My mother had lined up Daddy's contraband on the nightstand: besides the pipe in her hand, there were loose leaves of marijuana dumped from his jacket pockets, a couple of small white pills. Mom shook her head and melted onto the bed, defeated. Maybe Daddy had gotten tired of being on his best behavior. Or maybe he had never changed at all.

That night at dinner, Rebecca dragged her food across her plate and locked her sights full on Mom.

"Mommy, you're fat," she said flatly.

My bite of potato plopped back on my plate. Rebecca was lucky that Daddy wasn't here; that's the kind of rudeness that could set him flying off the handle and talking about belts.

"Rebecca Hall! That is not a nice thing to say!" Mom wheezed.

"But you *are* fat," Rebecca said again.

"Do you want me to tell your daddy what you said to me?"

"He's gonna leave you anyway. He told me so."

Then the room was quiet like the whole earth was holding its breath. It was the sucking sound of the air rushing over your head in a car crash, the sound the wind made when you were hurtling forward so fast that the speed of sound caught up to the speed of light, and that was the sound of everything breaking apart.

Jacob nodded into his plate.

"Daddy said he's moving into an apartment across the street, only you can't live there."

My mom's laughter cracked the quiet like a bat. It was not the kind of laugh where her belly shook and you wanted to laugh with her, it was the way witches in cartoons cackled while stirring big black pots full of hair and eyeballs.

"Eat your dinner," Mom said.

And I knew. I knew in that moment, as soon as Rebecca said, *Mommy you're fat*, that my mother was pregnant again. She was wearing the baggy clothes, she was breathing hard all the time. She was pregnant again, and that was why Daddy was leaving.

My father was probably smart not to confront Mom with the news himself; my parents hadn't had one of their explosive fights for almost a year; with all the anger they kept in check combined with the added tension of this pregnancy, somebody was likely to get shot. If my father had had the guts to talk to Mom about his decision, I imagine it would have gone something like this:

MICHAEL DECIDES[1]

For this reenactment, Michael should be played by Michael Keaton

---

[1] The scene works best if read aloud, ideally by two people. If you're alone, give it a shot. Or if you have a close friend at hand, share. If, on the other hand, you are on a train, plane, or otherwise beside a stranger, just use your imagination.

circa Working Stiffs; Peggy by Sally Field circa Norma Rae (with a few extra pounds on her). Both speak with thick New Jersey accents.

As directed by Quentin Tarantino

Michael, thirtyish, a little stoned, enters the kitchen, tosses his keys on the counter, and takes off his work boots. Pepé Le Pew–style fumes rise from his feet. Peggy, twenty-eight, her matronly chest barely contained by a faded nightgown, stirs a pot of ramen noodles on the stove.

PEGGY: Where's the milk?
MICHAEL: Am I wearing a shirt that says FRIGGIN' MILKMAN?"
PEGGY: You're the father; it's your job to get the milk.
MICHAEL: What's the matter, your tit broke?² The man brings
    home the friggin' bacon.

CLOSE ON: Michael's greasy thumb, popping the top off of a bottle of Grolsch, clink.

PEGGY: Well, we've been out of that for eight years. Last time
    you brought home bacon, Steve Perry was singing "Don't
    Stop Believin' " on WRAT.

CUT TO: The giant cauldron of ramen noodles as it bubbles.

MICHAEL: Frigging Journey. Bunch of freaks.

Beer backwashes up the neck of the bottle as Michael chugs it in one go. He BURPS.

---

2   Obviously, I would never speak about my own mother this way. But Tarantino might. Speak about somebody else's mother, I mean, not necessarily his *own* mother . . .

Michael slams the bottle on the counter.

MICHAEL: There was something I was going to tell you ... what the hell was it ...

Michael's face furrows. Peggy stirs the noodles.

MICHAEL: What the hell ... I was over at my mother's ... Danny dropped me off over here ... oh, yeah! We're friggin' through.

PEGGY: I think I missed that, what'd you say?

MICHAEL: I said, we're through. I can't deal with this crap anymore. Danny's waiting out front while I grab my shit. Good luck with the kids.

Michael reaches into the fridge for another frosty beer for the road.

PEGGY: You can't do this to me. How'm I supposed to feed three kids on three-thirty-five an hour?

Danny's El Camino honks loudly, twice.
Michael yells out the ripped screen, smacks the window frame.

MICHAEL: Hold your damn horses, Danny! I'm leaving my fuckin' family here!

Michael walks back to Peggy, runs his hands through his hair, collects his thoughts.

MICHAEL: A' right, Boo-Boo, listen. I'm going upstairs and get my shit. Then I'm leavin', and that'll be that.

Peggy's face remains placid. She ladles noodles into five chipped, mismatched bowls.

PEGGY: What about the kids?
MICHAEL: Oh. Yeah. That.

Michael sits down at the table to retrieve the Plan from the recesses of his brain.

MICHAEL: I'm taking the boy one, tomorrow morning my ma
is gonna come for one of the girls, then we'll send the last
one to your pops in Oklahoma. Or whatever.

Michael takes a drink of his beer; watches Peggy put the bowls on the table.

MICHAEL: You think your pops'll spring for the plane fare?

Michael screws his face together, thinking.

MICHAEL: Otherwise it's Greyhound all the way.
PEGGY: You can't put a six-year-old on a bus.
MICHAEL: What the hell? I'm the one doin' all the thinking
around here.
PEGGY: I already gave away three of these babies. You said the
last one would be the last one, and we'd move into a new
house and it'd just be the five of us. Now you want me to give
away all of them? I can't live with just me.
MICHAEL: Well I can't live with you, either. Boo-Boo, plans
change. The Lord came to me in my sleep last night, and
… it doesn't matter what He said, just, this is the only way.
A boy needs his father, and as it says in the Bible, when a
man—

BOOM.

Peggy pulls a .44 Magnum out of her cleavage and shoots Michael in the face. Blood splatters on the cracked beige walls. Michael's head lands face-first in the bowl of noodles.

PEGGY: Kids? Dinner!!!!!!!!!!!

END SCENE.

However Daddy delivered the news, though, our parents' split meant a world of changes for Jacob, Rebecca, and me. And if getting the message to my mom through one of their kids saved my daddy from getting shot in the head, I guess he picked the least stinky piece of that turd sandwich. Seems like he always did.

That night we stayed up until midnight watching reruns of *Cheers* in the living room. Mom was waiting for Daddy to return, and Jacob, Rebecca, and I were sticking close to Mom. We kept our ears perked for the jingle of keys in the back door, but Daddy didn't come home. Eventually, Mom said it was bedtime.

After Mom turned off the light in our bedroom, my siblings and I conferenced in whispers. While I was getting my ears pierced this afternoon, Daddy had told Jacob and Rebecca that he was filing for divorce and the three of us would have to be split up. Our father's plan was that I would be sent to live with his parents, Rebecca would go back to Oklahoma, and Jacob would stay on with our father in a smaller apartment across the street from where we lived now.

I bristled at the thought of being separated from Jacob and Rebecca. It had never crossed my mind that we might be separated the way our little sisters had been separated from us. I had never been alone like that before. The prospect of it made me feel like a turtle plucked from its shell.

"I'm not gonna," I said.

"Me, either," Rebecca said.

"Me, either," Jacob echoed.

We were a team. If Daddy wanted to leave, fine. Let him go. But I was not going to lose my sister again, or my brother.

I couldn't tell the precise moment when my sister and I transitioned from strangers to friends. It happened when we weren't paying attention. Over three months of sleeping in the same bed and playing the same games, we had gotten used to one another. And now we had a common cause to fight against. I couldn't imagine going back to living without her.

Across the room, Jacob rolled onto his stomach.

"We called Mimi and Granddad in Oklahoma City," he whispered. After Daddy told them about the decision, my brother and sister had walked six blocks to a pizzeria and placed a collect call to Oklahoma from the pay phone there.

"They said they'd have to talk to Mom. They want her to call them."

"They have the biggest house I've ever seen," Rebecca added.

She'd told us that the yard was a full acre, that the refrigerator had two doors, and that Mimi and Granddad had air-conditioning and cable and closets full of food. I didn't wonder if I'd like tromping around a one-acre backyard more than I enjoyed racing through the pavement of the neighborhood. New Jersey was the only place I knew; I couldn't imagine that anywhere in the world could be different from here. Rebecca said the situation in Oklahoma was good, so I believed her.

Mom's relationship with her father and stepmother had always been a bear. I'd heard her tell her friends how her father used to lock her out of the house when she broke her curfew, so she would sleep under the pine tree in the front yard until her father came out for the morning paper. *Wanted to let him worry*, she said. And she must have had a reason to run away from their house when she was seventeen. But regardless of my mother's past there, Jacob, Rebecca, and I knew that the three of us would fit in our grandparents' house in Oklahoma. They could afford to keep us together. The biggest question was, would they? And would our mother let us go?

Setting our plan into motion was complicated. For Mimi and Granddad to talk to her, Peggy would have to call them, since we still didn't have a phone for them to call her. That call would open a whole can of worms about what Mom had promised when she took Rebecca back three months ago. Her father might dig deep enough to find out about the baby girls that she had relinquished for adoption. They might discover that she was, in fact, pregnant right now, and that it was the pressure of this baby that drove her husband away again.

AS THE sun rose the next morning, the house was silent. Mom hadn't roused herself, so Jacob cooked breakfast and Rebecca and I tucked ourselves around the glass-top table in the dining room. Through the wall I could hear Jacob scraping a pan of sizzling eggs. I pressed my palms onto the gray glass tabletop. The heat from my body steamed an impression on the glass for a moment before the air caught it and swept it away. When the sun rose high enough I could see the greasy remains of hundreds of old handprints, Jacob's and Rebecca's and mine layered all together from the many times we had sat around this table waiting for something to happen, pressing our handprints down and watching them disappear like smoke.

This was the way our lives had always gone. Change was the only constant I knew. Things changed and we were always somehow fine. I had not been confronted yet with the idea that luck, like daddies, can run out when you least expect it.

Jacob covered our fried eggs with neon slices of American cheese and we buzzed over our plates about events that were likely to happen. It was a meditation, so we would be prepared for anything and would know what plan to throw our joint weight behind.

MOM CAME downstairs, and neighbor women came over, offering not so much plans as condolences. They called Michael the names that my mother couldn't, *asshole, burnout, lazy, jackass, hippie, fuckup, liar, liar, liar.*

"I thought maybe we could keep this baby," Peggy said. "Maybe we'd do the whole thing like we did when Jacob was born. Maybe we'd be okay."

My mom dragged more and more visibly as the day progressed. She was like a house without electricity; still standing, but dark inside. Meanwhile, Jacob, Rebecca, and I pulled out every toy we owned to distract ourselves from the spooky silence in the house. As the days turned into a week, we attempted to do the laundry. School was starting soon and we'd have to get ourselves ready. We got as far as piling all the dirty laundry into stacks in the living room and then took a twenty-four-hour break because no one was brave enough to venture into the basement.

The apartment looked like every closet and drawer had vomited its contents down the stairs and into the living room. The TV blared cartoons, Jacob made us toast when we were hungry.

Mom went up to her bedroom to rest a lot. We were supposed to think that she was cleaning, but it was obvious from the paths that wound down the stairs and to the kitchen that no one had been cleaning here for a while. I had no way of understanding the desolation she must have felt at the blunt knowledge that this family was not enough to convince my father to stay. To my mother, his willful absence was an indictment: She was unlovable. Maybe we all were. It was a thought that was so overwhelming, my mind refused to acknowledge it.

Then one afternoon, a week into our limbo, there was a knock at the door. I cast around for a place to hide. Unexpected knocks were always bad news. I snuck behind the door as Jacob opened it.

"Oh, hi!" he said to a woman in a trench coat.

Rebecca leapt from the back of the sofa and hugged that woman like a lion hugging a piece of steak. The lady had gray hair curled just so, she wore leather driving gloves that coordinated with her coat and sunglasses on top of her head perched behind big rose-petal ears. She saw me staring at her.

"Hello, Mary."

I took her hand when she offered it and felt all the little bones creak inside it.

"This is Mimi," Rebecca said.

"You remember me," Mimi told me.

So the woman who had rescued Rebecca in 1983 was here in my living room again. She was as businesslike and unruffled as I had always imagined, though she was less blond and more gray-haired than I remembered from our very brief meeting years ago. It was as if we had conjured her. Mom was pale and strange as a beached jellyfish when Jacob dragged her downstairs. When she saw Mimi, though, the look on her face was unmistakable; it was relief.

Mimi didn't dwell on the mess we had ceased to notice; she got things done. She laid her coat and gloves across the arm of the sofa and said, "Let's clean this place up and get some dinner."

The next day, she rustled my father out of whatever hole he'd been hiding in and brought him home for a sit-down.

I was racing down the stairs that afternoon when I slid around the doorway into the dining room and ran right into the adults' pow-wow.

"Hey, come here, Pumpkin!" I heard over my shoulder.

My father was sitting in the far corner, behind the gray glass table, which had been cleaned of all our sticky handprints. Mimi stood by the window, and Mom hovered in the kitchen. Everyone in the room knew my father was in trouble but him. He reached into his pocket.

"I almost forgot your allowance." He waved a dollar bill at me.

"What's allowance?"

"It's for doing your chores." He grinned.

"What's chores?"

"You cleaned your room."

"When?"

"Two weeks ago."

Did I?

"No, I didn't!"

He threw his head back and laughed up to the ceiling. I had no idea I was so hilarious. But I wasn't an idiot, so I took the dollar and slipped out of the room.

On the front porch, Jacob and Rebecca were sitting on the step grabbing fragments of broken concrete and pitching them into the yard.

"Did he give you a dollar?" Jacob asked me.

I nodded.

"Let's get some candy, then."

Normally I would have saved this dollar in the pencil case under my bed where I kept the seven dollars in pennies that I had won at a church picnic, but that would mean going back in the house where my daddy was getting in trouble and laughing about it.

Today felt like the world could end at any moment, and we had three whole dollars between us, so what was the point of having a savings? We bought butterscotch Krimpets, Dr Pepper, M&M's, Reese's Pieces, and Fun Dips, and took our candy haul to the parking lot of the school around the corner from our apartment. Close enough to the house that we could hear anyone yelling for us, but far enough away that we didn't have to be seen.

"She's probably telling him that he's got to stick around."

"She looked mad."

"No . . . sad."

If it came down to it, the three of us knew the nooks and crannies of this neighborhood better than any grown person, so if the negotiations went the wrong way we had a catalog of abandoned sheds, empty dugouts, and alleyways at our disposal. My seven-dollar stash of pennies could keep us afloat for a couple of days at least.

TWO WEEKS later, soon after school started, Mom and Mimi broke the news to us that Jacob, Rebecca, and I were going to Oklahoma with Mimi. It was what we wanted and now it was happening. It felt inevitable, unstoppable; not at all the way I expected.

No legal papers had been drawn up to transfer custody to Mimi when she scooped up my sister in 1983. When my mother returned for her child, it was impossible for Mimi to say no. But this time around, if Mimi and Granddad were going to help, they had terms. If they were going to take the three of us under their wing, they'd need custody granted to them. They'd need a piece of paper to get us enrolled in schools and listed on Granddad's insurance, something that would make it possible for them say no next time. After another week to get all the paperwork in order, we were off. Still, Mimi and Mom promised that the arrangement was temporary, just until one of our parents could get back on their feet enough to bring all three of us back.

We didn't have a lot of luggage. Most of our clothes and toys were too ratty to bother packing. We'd figure it out when we got to Oklahoma, Mimi said.

In the plane, I sat next to my brother. Mimi and Rebecca were across the aisle and one row back. My feet stuck straight out in front of me. Mimi gave me a stick of gum at the airport so I could chew it and my ears wouldn't pop when we got in the air.

As we left behind the salty humidity of New Jersey, a flight attendant handed me a packet of peanuts. I was entering a world where people handed me things when I needed them, where I got the things I wished for. I no longer had to worry about where my next meal would come from, and I was done, too, with the concern about how I would stay attached to my brother and sister. I'd no longer have to watch my mother for the signs that she was falling apart.

It was in that moment of emptiness when we reached a cruising altitude and I was neither in New Jersey nor yet in Oklahoma that I finally felt it, the donkey kick to the ribs that only a great loss can give a person. I had never been away from my mother. Not once in my life had I gone an entire day without seeing her. Now I'd have to live without her. The woman who understood everything I meant to say, who let me bury her face with her hair so I could dig her out again. The woman whom I didn't let hold my hand when I got my ears pierced because I'd thought I was too grown up. I didn't feel grown up now. I wanted my mommy more than I had wanted anything in my life.

It's only temporary, I reminded myself. I didn't know how long temporary was, but I did know that it was not forever.

I stared out the window, past my brother's head. I had been excited to distraction about getting on an airplane because I was certain that once I was above the cloud cover I would see where the Care Bears lived. If I could get their attention, if they saw my brother, sister, and me in transit like this, the Care Bears would scoop us up, bellies blazing with rainbow light, and fix our fractured family. Or maybe the Care Bears would let us live with them in the clouds where there weren't any grown-ups to muck up our lives. That might be the best of everything.

PART TWO

oklahoma

1989–2000

Reflections

imi herded my siblings and me off the plane and through the airport arrivals gate at the Will Rogers World Airport in Oklahoma City. At the end of the skyway stood my grandfather, the man my mother had run away from so many years ago. He wore tan trousers and a periwinkle button-front shirt that made the blue in his blue-gray eyes stand out.

Granddad was immediately different from the daddies I had seen before. Standing at five feet eleven inches, he was the tallest man I'd seen in person. When he enlisted in the Air Force at the age of seventeen—before age compressed his bones—he was probably a full six feet. He was broad-shouldered and bifocaled, with a belly that spilled slightly over his belt. The sheer amount of space he took up demanded my attention. His silver hair was parted deep on the right side and tastefully combed back. It was the same hairstyle he'd worn since he was a child in the 1940s in Philadelphia. In addition to his wedding band and a large silver watch, Granddad wore an enormous garnet ring on his right hand; the stone was bigger than his knuckles. When our group reached him, he kissed Mimi on the forehead, then methodically hiked up the legs of his trousers before squatting down and wrapping Rebecca in a bear hug. He wrapped Jacob and me in a second, shared hug, then turned to the business of tracking down our luggage.

Granddad's eyes darted to television screens that told where each flight's bags could be found. "It says carousel number two, but we'll see . . ." he said, already bracing himself for things to deviate from his plan. The walk to baggage claim was punctuated with Granddad's sporadic exhalations as he struggled under the weight of the many things he could say right now, but wouldn't.

We collected our few small bags—from carousel four, not two. Granddad shook his head because he hated to be right about these things. Then we climbed into his shiny Chrysler. I worried that I was sullying its light gray upholstery by simply breathing on it. I was careful not to brush my shoes on the seat and leave a stain.

As we drove toward Mimi and Granddad's house, Rebecca chirped out the names of the streets we took.

"Interstate 40!"

"Twenty-ninth Street!"

"Grand Boulevard!"

Granddad rumbled from the driver's seat, "What street do we take to get home?" and my sister said, "McKinley Avenue!"

I could only see the upper half of this new world as it crawled slowly past my window. The few trees I could make out were short and fat and wind-burned. Without tall buildings or trees to frame it, the sky filled my view like an ocean.

Jacob dug his elbow deep into my side when the Chrysler pulled into the brick driveway of the house on Forty-fourth Street. I sucked in my breath. The house was built into a hill on an acre of land in the middle of the city. In a state that had so far looked like a flat moonscape, Mimi and Granddad had found a spot that was covered with trees and topography.

Two collies rushed to the chain-link fence as the car came to a stop. When they saw Rebecca step out of the car, the dogs jumped on each other's backs and fought to be the first to lick her hands through the fence.

The house was two and half stories, gray with white trim. Granddad pushed a giant wooden front door open and the air-conditioned air turned the sweat on my skin into goose bumps. From the main entryway, the first floor of the house split into three rooms: the living room to the right, Granddad's den to the left, the dining room straight ahead. Between Granddad's den and the dining room a staircase led to the second floor, which contained only the attic and one bedroom. Past the dining room were two bedrooms, two bathrooms, and the kitchen. Beneath the preserving effects of the central air-conditioning was the hint of lemon polish, window cleaner, and the toasty aroma of wall-to-wall carpet that had been recently vacuumed.

Mimi glided through the rooms with the fluency of a native, delicately removing her driving gloves finger by finger and laying them on the edge of the dining room table. She wore driving gloves whenever she left the house, regardless of season. The compression helped relieve her arthritis, and when she was a girl people always wore hats and gloves in public. She hung her coat in the hall closet and said, "Girls sleep downstairs and boys upstairs," as if saying boys in the plural would soften the fact that Jacob would have to sleep in a room all by himself.

The attic bedroom had a brass daybed pushed against one wall as an excuse to call it a guest room, but its official purpose was to act as the way station for things that Mimi couldn't decide if she wanted to keep. Having grown up during the Great Depression, she never discarded anything until she was certain that she didn't have a use for it. She tucked items upstairs to keep Granddad from throwing them out before she was ready to part with them. There was a black-and-white TV with rabbit-ear antennae, a giant wooden hope chest full of quilts, translucent christening gowns, and slippery silk kimonos that had been gifts from Granddad when he was stationed overseas. In the corner by the heating vent was a conical, stainless steel hair dryer—the kind that looked like a helmet—that once lived in the beauty shop that Mimi had owned in the 1950s. This room was where my mother slept before she ran away. The nameplate on the door still read Peggy's Room.

The house was built in 1922 and had belonged to Mimi's parents. Its original location was across town, fifteen miles away. Mimi had already owned the large corner lot on Forty-fourth Street on the southwest side of the city, so when her parents gave her their old house—the perfect house fifteen miles from the perfect piece of land—Mimi hired men to pick the house up and move it. They had to take down traffic lights along the route to get the house across major intersections. There were photographs of it in the local paper. She hired another string of men to build a foundation for the house by cutting into the hill. This added a half story underneath the property, and when the house arrived, that dugout became Mimi's basement workshop, where she made porcelain dolls.

Every exterior wall of the house, both upstairs and downstairs, was covered in banks of windows, but they were shrouded with floor-to-ceiling drapes, the heavy kind, faced with plastic blackout backing that blocked the sun. The overall effect was like walking into a cave: cool and dark, with shadows clinging to the high corners, hiding all manner of menacing things.

Every piece of furniture had permanence to it, details from another era—clawed feet, dark woods, brass fittings. Things crafted and carved before the distractions of basic cable, Internet, or telephones, when you could get workmanship, when people knew and cared about the difference between an English dovetail and a French one. In the months to come, I'd learn that this house needed constant care. It required the taking down of drapes and washing them, wrapping brooms with dampened dish towels to clean ceilings, soft rags greased with lemon oil to polish window frames. Mimi didn't get this far having nice things by not taking care of them.

Mimi, Granddad, and Rebecca fanned out through the house. Jacob and I stopped at the edge of the dining room, unsure where to begin. The dining room and hallways were lined with china presses whose glass fronts were so sparkling clean they reflected the rooms of the house back at you. As if placed strategically, they bounced reflections around corners and through the whole house. Standing at the edge of the dining room, Jacob and I could see Mimi rummaging through dresser drawers in the back bedroom, Granddad taking off his watch in the front bedroom, and Rebecca disappearing through the doorway of what must be a walk-in closet.

"Come on, now, brush your teeth, and then bed," Mimi said from the other room, her ghostly face looking directly at us through the glass of the cabinet in front of us.

I scrambled through the hallway, following the path I saw my sister take. I stopped short when I saw myself in the glass door of Mimi's doll cabinet. The girl looking back at me was shocking.

People calling me Punky and Pumpkin all my life had led me to believe I was ruddy and round, but the reflection in the glass was bony as a skeleton. Elbows and knees protruded like horns from my skinny arms and legs, my hair frizzed around my head with a will of its own. Mixed with my freckles were weird bruises that I didn't remember getting. My hands were floppy and big as flippers. I searched my face for something that matched the image I had of myself in my head, but nothing squared up.

Beyond my reflection, in the cabinet itself was a pair of chestnut-haired dolls—a boy and a girl—holding Easter baskets. They were the first two dolls Mimi had sculpted by hand. "I based them off of pictures that Peggy sent me of you and your brother," she said as she walked past me into the kitchen and began laying out bowls and juice glasses for tomorrow's breakfast. The dolls didn't look anything like us. They were dressed in starched clothes with serene expressions on their faces. Neat caps of hair framed their faces. The only things that looked right were the strips of tape on their hands where Mimi'd had to reattach fingers that had fallen off.

The bedroom in New Jersey where my siblings and I had planned our rescue seemed like another life now. When we were whispering about Oklahoma I didn't know it would be so different or that I would feel so strange. I didn't know about nice furniture and reflections, about dogs and yards and a sky so big and a land so flat and a Granddad so quiet; a place that was home to them but not to me. I wished more than anything that I could close my eyes and be back in New Jersey with my mother, falling asleep in the nest of her arms and listening to the lullaby of passing cars. *That* was my home. I wanted to scratch out the window screens and scream and cry and hightail it back to New Jersey, but it was too far and too dark and I was too small and I couldn't.

I crossed through the downstairs bedroom that Rebecca and I would share and into the bathroom, where my brother and sister were huddled around the sink. There were three kid-sized toothbrushes in a plastic cup on the counter; Granddad must have picked them up before we arrived. I imagined his broad-shouldered frame in a drugstore aisle, holding these child-sized accessories in his massive paws, his garnet ring clicking against the blister packs. Like the rest of the house, the bathroom was covered in deep shag carpet because Mimi was always cold. The thought of her feet touching cold tile or wood floors for even a moment was unthinkable; it was her house, after all.

A nightgown was laid out for me on Rebecca's and my queen-sized bed. It matched the one my sister wore. Mimi glided into the room and clasped her hands together, announcing, "It's time for little boys to go upstairs now," and ushered my brother out of the room. We didn't even say a proper good night. I slipped into my nightgown. It was brand-new, with bell-like ruffles around the wrists and a wide ruffle skimming the floor. Rebecca's gown had blue flowers and mine had pink. This was the first occurrence of what would become a pattern of dressing Rebecca and me in identical outfits of different colors. I wondered if Jacob had brand-new pajamas on his bed, too. I wondered if he was happy to have his own room, if he was relieved to not have to worry about me anymore.

My new bedroom had three windows covered in forest-green crushed velvet drapes. The carpet was the same deep green and the walls were covered in shiny gold wallpaper printed with autumn leaves. It was like being inside a jewelry box.

Mimi tucked Rebecca and me under the sheets. She lingered for a moment on Rebecca's side of the bed, brushing my sister's long hair back from her forehead and squeezing her hands.

"Are you happy to be home?" Mimi asked, and Rebecca nodded with such enthusiasm that my stomach flopped against my ribs. Mimi kissed my sister on top of her head and squeezed Rebecca as tight as her arthritis would allow, then rose to turn off the lights. "Good night girls," she said as the room became dark as coal.

On this first night, my unease made me good. I didn't roll over to Rebecca's side of the bed and smack her arm. I didn't kick her in the back. In the bed that we had shared in New Jersey, my sister and I were close enough that I could wrap my arms around her like a doll. But this new bed was so big that when I stretched my arms and legs out as far as I could, my limbs connected to nothing.

I lay awake long after my sister's breathing told me she was asleep. The wind moaned outside like something dying. The stress of Rebecca knowing all the street names that I'd never heard, of the house watching me, of my brother so far away and my mother even farther . . . I was squashed under the weight of it all, and I buried my wet face in the pillow. I cried because of the strangeness of this place, because I was afraid of the dark, because I was relieved, because I didn't know how any of this was going to unfold.

I wiggled my feet under the covers out of habit. I used to do this to keep myself awake until my mom came home from her night shift at the fast-food place, but this act soothed me in a different way tonight. It was not so much a distraction to keep me awake as it was a connection to my *me-ness*, a reminder that I was still myself. Even in these pink pajamas in this big bed in this big house in this flat state, I was myself and I was in one piece. I was still my mother's daughter, my brother's sister, my sisters' sister, still Mary. Nothing had changed except my address.

Telling Stories

W hurr you frum?"

A blue-eyed boy stood beside the tetherball pole, absently smacking the stringed ball so it bounced against the metal. The schoolyard was packed with kids in scratchy coats hollering at one another in voices that twanged like a chorus of banjos. Mimi dropped us off here at the yard in front of the elementary school just minutes before and my brother and sister immediately got swept into groups of kids their age. Jacob raced another boy across the monkey bars and Rebecca giggled with a girl she remembered from Vacation Bible School a couple of summers ago. My brother and sister were joiners.

I stood by the bike rack and stared at my saddle oxfords, waiting to be let inside the school building. I was hoping that no one would see me, but it was as if my wishing so hard to be invisible made me the opposite.

It was our first day.

"Frickle-Fayce, I'm talkin' tuh you! Whurr you come frum?" the boy asked again, shouting louder because he refused to come any closer to me.

It was gray and cloudy. Other kids were looking now. I suddenly realized he was talking to me. I kept my eyes on my shoes.

"New Jersey," I said.

"New Jersey?" he said. "Yer a dirty Yankee, then." He spat on the ground. The tetherball's metal fittings clanged together.

"No, I'm not," I said. I didn't know what a Yankee was, but it didn't sound good.

"Yeah, ya' are," he insisted, "an' a *liberal*, too, I reckon." The word *liberal* drew another fat plop of spit from the back of his throat.

Before I was forced to admit that I didn't know what a liberal was, either, a girl in a navy coat rang a large bell from the top of the school steps. The other kids scrambled into lines behind poles that I now saw had signs affixed to their fronts: Ms. ULAK'S FIRST GRADE, MR. NOBLE'S THIRD GRADE. I was in the same line as this blue-eyed spitter, for Mrs. Morris's second grade.

We filed into our classroom and removed coats and Mrs. Morris—a stout woman with a blond bob—called from behind her desk, "Where is our new student, Mary King?" I froze for a moment, because the chance that there was another new Mary in this room was slim, but Mary King was not my name. It was my first name with my grandfather's surname tacked on. I stopped breathing for a second, floating in the possibility that maybe I was not supposed to be here after all, that I would be revealed as an impostor who had not, in fact, earned a spot in this classroom, an impostor who was very likely a *Yankee*.

Mrs. Morris's eyes fell on me and she hustled me to a desk. "There you are! Mary just moved here all the way from New Jersey!" Her smile cracked her face into rivers and tributaries. "All y'all make her feel real welcome, all right?"

The blue-eyed boy from the playground pointed his finger at me like a gun and shot me from across the room.

I DECIDED to keep my mouth shut for the rest of the day, until I was back at the house on Forty-fourth Street.

Once there, I moved directly to my newly discovered favorite spot: the patch of carpet underneath the dining room table. It was one of the only places in the house where, once inside it, the reflections couldn't detect me. I crawled through the carved wooden table legs and slid the heavy chairs in behind me so I could disappear. That was the clearest motivation I had, to disappear. It was nothing like a full-blown death wish, nothing so dramatic, it was more ephemeral. I wanted to fade into the shadows and exist without such inconveniences as a physical body. A physical body needed things, to be tended, to be touched, to be fed. A body could hurt, which I did when I thought about it, so I preferred not to think about it at all. I preferred to lie beneath the dining room table with the heavy wooden chairs pulled close around me, my limbs threaded through their legs, and imagine what it would be like to be the wind. To blow over the earth, miles and miles, tied to nothing and no one, never feeling lost or angry or hurt. Never feeling anything. To be a ghost, to sink into walls like a drop of rain when it hits the ocean and transforms from one solitary raindrop into ocean. I wanted to be everywhere and nowhere, to be anything but human, anything but a child.

My body was here in Oklahoma, but some aspect of me hadn't made it to the new location. In the neighborhood tribe in New Jersey, I knew what to want and how to get it. The constellations that I had learned to navigate by in my short seven-year life—my mother, the Other Mothers, the daddies and the sound of the Pinto backfiring into the alley behind the house, the kids with

bats and leg braces and the too-close neighbors—now had no rel-
evance. I had learned a language that was useless.

I didn't have a vocabulary to explain this feeling to anyone
around me. I was afraid that if I tried to describe it, Mimi and
Granddad would think I was bad. Maybe they would send me
back. Part of me longed to return to New Jersey and to my
mother, but I feared that I would be sent without my brother and
sister. It was a fear that I absorbed over the many years I had seen
my sisters sent away, one that grew larger when I was sent away
myself. I had been a willing participant in my relocation, but I
knew that I would have been sent here even if I hadn't wanted to
go, that I was a person who could be shipped off on a whim.

We were halfway through dinner that night when I took a
deep breath and asked, "What's a Yankee?"

Mimi said, "It's a person from the Northeast."

But Granddad wanted to know where I'd heard that word.

I told him about the Spitter and he harrumphed. "Some of
these Okies think the Civil War is still going on. We're all Yan-
kees here, except Mimi-Mouse," he continued, his eyes glittering
mischievously as he winked at his wife. "But you don't mind, do
you?" He squeezed her knee under the table.

"Not so long as you worsh your feet," Mimi said.

From time to time she'd slip into the same banjo-twang as the
kids from the schoolyard. It only popped up with certain words
and turns of phrase, like *worsh* instead of wash, *Missour-ah* instead
of Missouri. Then there were the phrases like "hide and watch,"
which was a warning (*You kids keep getting out of a bed, and you can
hide and watch what happens*); "we don't need to be entertained,"
which meant hush (*Finish your dinner, we don't need to be entertained*);
and "telling stories," which meant bald-faced lying (*Don't tell me
any stories, now . . .*).

Our plates were nearly clean when Mimi looked sidelong at my brother. "You're watching that TV upstairs after bedtime," she accused, folding her hands in her lap. Jacob said that he was not.

"Nobody likes a storyteller."

There it was.

"I can hear you moving around up there at night," she continued.

"I'm *not*," he insisted.

"Charles, what do you think?" Mimi turned to Granddad for backup.

Granddad adjusted his glasses, thinking. "I think you need to write, *I will not lie*, one hundred times before you go to bed tonight, young man."

I had a sense that this was a test designed to show all of us at the table who was in charge of the house, who was omniscient, omnipotent, and omnipresent, and who was NOT. Mimi nodded softly, and it was clear that Granddad had passed with high marks.

I'd never known my brother to be a liar, but if I knew anything for sure, it was that Mimi heard every squeaking floorboard and saw every reflection in this house. Maybe my brother was, in fact, telling stories. I tried to catch Jacob's eye but he stared at his plate, no doubt wondering over the words *one hundred sentences*, feeling how impossibly dreary it would be to write them all before bedtime.

IN ADDITION to Jacob's lying, Mimi set her sights on me and my shyness. It was another thing that simply would not do.

One afternoon in early November, Mimi took Jacob, Rebecca, and me to a library after school. I slipped into the silence like it

was a well-worn winter coat. The Young Readers section was a
sunken room sprinkled with tuffets and various child-sized nooks
scooped into the brick walls. I'd never read a book without pictures. Mimi glided through the aisles and snapped up *Little House
in the Big Woods*, *Anne of Green Gables*, and *Little Women*.

When we arrived home, Mimi left the stack of books on the
dining room table. I waited until I saw her back disappear into the
kitchen before I made my move to dive under it. The phone rang.

Mimi and Granddad had three rotary-dial phones spread
throughout the house and one wireless phone in the basement.
Their tinny ringing jangled my nerves and forced my tongue
against the roof of my mouth until someone picked up the
receiver. Not knowing who was on the other end of line, I avoided
answering the phone myself. Jacob and Rebecca, however, loved
nothing better than answering the phone. This time Rebecca got
it first.

"King residence!" she chirped into the phone. "Hi, Mom," she
said after a beat. Through the table legs I saw my sister's plump
calves lift from the floor and dangle from the chair by the phone.
Jacob stood close, fidgeting to be next.

Once I knew it was my mother on the other end of the line,
my hunger for hearing her voice sent me scrambling out of my
hiding place and fidgeting alongside my brother.

Mom was more my mom than she was Rebecca's mom, and
in those interminable minutes when my sister was talking to *my*
mom I was wild with rage. I could have ripped that receiver out
of her soft pink hand and kicked her out of the chair down to the
floor. I didn't, but I knew I was capable of it.

Mimi strutted in from the kitchen with a timer in her hand.
"You each get ten minutes," she said and set the timer ticking.

"You two wait over here." She nudged me and Jacob—more with her expression than with her hands—three feet away from Rebecca and the telephone. She didn't want to hear any fussing and she didn't want us to hang up the phone when we were done; she wanted to talk to our mother. Then she left and the three of us had to self-police.

When it was my turn on the phone, my mother said, "Hello, my Mary!" and the sound of her voice devastated me. She sounded exactly as I remembered her, but coming through the receiver directly into my ear she was both closer to me and farther from me than ever before. "Hello?" she said again, and I managed to say, "Hi, Mommy." What I wanted was for my ten minutes to be filled to overflowing with my mother's voice running and spilling together words; I didn't even care what they were. I wanted to deposit all of those words, all of her voice, inside me like pennies in a bank that I could draw from later. But this was a conversation, and I had to keep up my end. It never occurred to me that my mother might be wishing for the same thing from me, for me to burble like a brook overfilling our conversations with new things I had learned.

She asked me if I was being good, and I nodded, of course I was.

"Meems?" my mother asked. "Are you still there?"

"She's nodding!" Jacob hollered toward the phone, looking over his shoulder to see if Mimi was watching him.

"I'm nodding," I said into the receiver.

And then the timer dinged and my time was up. I handed the receiver to Jacob and crawled back under the table, to think about what I would sound like when I became the wind and how long it would take me to blow all the way to New Jersey.

I was just pulling my ankle under the table when Mimi called from the kitchen.

"Mary, would you come in here, please?" Using the reflections bounced from the gleaming breakfront and onto the glass cabinet in the hallway, she must have seen me. I wondered if I would be made to write one hundred times, *I will not hide under tables*.

"Bring me one of my books, please?"

I slid a book off the top of the dining table and bobbed into the kitchen, where Mimi was expertly sculpting hamburger into perfectly spherical meatballs.

"You can read, can't you?"

I nodded.

"Out loud?

I nodded slowly.

"That's good, 'cause I can't read while I've got my hands in this bowl. Hop in that chair and read to me, would you?"

I tucked myself into the chair in the corner by the refrigerator and took a deep breath and began to read.

"A little louder, please? I can't hear you over the water boiling," Mimi said.

The timer sounded in the dining room and Mimi washed her hands. "I'll be right back, don't read on ahead, now," she said as she went toward the phone in the hallway. She might have winked at me. It's possible that was a wink, but it could have been the light playing a trick.

I tried not to read ahead, so I flipped through the pictures instead. Two little girls batting a balloon back and forth, a wild-haired girl cradling a rough-looking doll in a cabin. A big bearded father pulling on his boots.

Over dinner I was full of questions. How do you build

a cabin, where is Wisconsin, is a bear bigger than Granddad, and how much bigger? I was fascinated. Something inside me switched on when I picked up that book. I couldn't wait to keep reading.

A week later at school, our phonics lesson was interrupted by sirens. The school secretary announced over the intercom that this was only a drill, but we were still meant to take it seriously.

"It's a tore-nado drill, Yankee," the Spitter said in my ear.

"I *know*," I said. But I didn't know; no one had bothered to explain tornadoes to me.

"You don't have tore-nadoes in New Jersey," he insisted, falling directly behind me in line.

"We have hurricanes, and they are *way* worse," I barked back as we marched into the hallway, hugging the windowless walls while the sirens bleated overhead.

"No, they ain't," he said as we crouched against the wall, our laced-together fingers covering our necks. It was the precise position we took during hurricane drills in New Jersey. This fact emboldened me.

"They are so. I knew a girl who *died* in a hurricane," I hissed at the Spitter around my elbow.

This statement was absolutely untrue. But the spooked look in the Spitter's eyes told me that I'd got him. He turned his whole face toward me, elbows wrapped like elephant ears around his head. "What happened?" he asked.

Of course he wanted to know what had happened. I was curious, too. How could I have lived through a hurricane that had killed a classmate? How would I have a story like that? A story big enough to haunt, but small enough to avoid being national news? I had wandered too far into this lie to back out gracefully. I had to figure out a way through it. For the briefest of moments I was struck dumb. But then it came to me.

I closed my eyes and saw my former classroom in New Jersey; I heard the sirens, smelled the chalk and humid air. I saw myself filing into the hallway with my classmates. Mixed in with everyone else was an imagined girl. A hazel-eyed girl . . . She was unimpressed by the warning signs all around her and ducked into the girls' bathroom on the first floor. She thought the alarm was just another drill, thought that maybe she'd sneak out the window when no one was looking and run over to Mr. Ed's bodega and buy herself some Skittles. She could taste the sugary syrupy goodness already. Her mouth watered.

But that was her mistake.

Because this time the drill was *real.*

In the hallway in Oklahoma, the Spitter's face was slack-jawed and guileless. He believed me. I told him how the hazel-eyed girl climbed onto the radiator to boost herself out the window, how she couldn't have seen the wind pick up a tree and send it crashing through the glass. How the girl was crushed to the cold tile floor.

"She was killed on impact," I said, like I'd heard in crime shows back when my mom let me watch them with her. I shook my head. Killed on impact.

"That's awful," he whispered.

I nodded.

I knew there was nothing worse than a story where a kid disappears.

Discipline

We had only been in Oklahoma a few months when the truth came barreling out and ruined everything. It was the night after we talked to our mother, my brother said, over his plate of spaghetti, that Mom told him she had found a nice family for the baby. It was the same family that adopted baby Meghan.

Dinner paused. Forks suspended in mid-bite.

"What baby?" Granddad asked.

"The new baby. The one that isn't born yet. Mom's giving her to another family. Like the other babies," said Jacob.

"What other babies?" Granddad said.

"The . . . other babies. Lisa and Rebekah Two and Meghan." Redness crept up his neck like a quickly advancing allergic reaction.

"That's enough. There are no other babies. There's just the three of you."

"But there are—"

"That's impossible," Mimi said, as she unblinkingly sliced her pasta noodles with a knife. "I was just there, Charles, I would have known."

Granddad, however, didn't look so sure.

"Now that you've upset everybody's dinner, you can be excused from the table," Mimi said to my brother.

"And before you go to bed tonight," she continued, "I'll need two hundred sentences from you. *I will not tell stories.* Two hundred times. Go on, now."

Jacob spent the next couple hours before bed alone in the upstairs bedroom while Rebecca rolled on the TV room carpet in front of Granddad's recliner yelling, "Buy a vowel!" and I pretended to do homework until it was time for us to put on our pajamas and line up for good-nights. My brother arrived for the good-night scene with five sheets of paper in hand. Granddad inspected them through the bottom of his bifocals.

"Did you learn your lesson?" Granddad asked.

"Yeah." My brother tried to keep his eyes off the floor.

"Don't say, *Yeah. Yeah* is not an answer. Say, *Yes, sir,* or *No, sir.* Do you understand?"

"Yes, sir," my brother puffed.

My brother didn't cry like most people do. When he was little he had problems with his tear ducts and had to have them removed. Even though his tear-making apparatus worked fine now, something in him hung on to that old wound, and when he got upset he didn't produce tears. His eyes got red, and the redness spread down his face. His dry waterworks always led adults to think he was faking. I knew he wasn't, but I didn't say anything in my brother's defense.

That night, I lay wide awake in the big queen bed, feeling the earth shift beneath me while my sister softly snored. As glad as I was that I didn't have to write sentences, I wished that I had jumped in at the dinner table. I wished I had said that my brother was right, that we were both there when it happened and it was true. But I didn't. Maybe the habit of keeping a secret for so long was impossible to overcome. Once it was hanging in the air, and my brother was being branded a liar, I couldn't shout out in his defense. We were supposed to be a team. Wherever my brother was, I was supposed to be right by his side. But this place, this house with its upstairs and downstairs, these people with their *yes, sirs* and *no, sirs*, with their books, backyards, and plates of pasta dinners had twisted my allegiance. I was the one who lied, with my story about the girl in the hurricane. My brother had told the truth. He got the punishment I deserved, but there was nothing I could do about it.

Things went on like that for months. Even after a phone call with Peggy confirmed the existence of our long-lost sisters, my brother was not able to shake Mimi's perception that he was a liar. Our parents had kept this secret for years and had drawn Jacob into their cover story; it made sense that perhaps my brother had inherited the art of deception from them. And it was Mimi and Granddad's responsibility to exorcise it from him. With each perceived transgression Mimi and Granddad crafted sentences with cause-and-effect, with multiple clauses, definitions of things.

On the weekends Jacob was tasked with picking up fallen tree limbs in the yard before Granddad attacked the lawn with a riding mower. As a boy who'd grown up surrounded by pavement, Jacob never had honed a skill for identifying sticks tangled in fields of grass. Frequently he missed some and had to be reminded that a branch could damage the blades of the lawn mower, or could go flying through the blades and put somebody's eye out, or could stall the mower.

None of these things actually occurred—Granddad always

saw the branches himself before he mowed over them—but they could have. And because they could have, Jacob had to write, *I will always be conscientious in my chores to ensure the safety of everyone involved.*

On a random Tuesday night when Mimi was certain that my brother had not, in fact, brushed his teeth—she said she checked his toothbrush and it wasn't wet—he wrote, *I will practice good hygiene every day,* followed by a full copy of the definition of *hygiene* out of the Merriam-Webster dictionary. Two hundred and fifty times each. If at any time Jacob protested these assignments, a few hundred *I will remember that I am an example to my younger sisters and will not talk back when I am being disciplined*'s were tacked on.

There was something genteel about writing sentences as a means of discipline. Though the steeliness in Mimi's voice when she assigned them suggested that there were more terrible penalties if my brother did not comply.

So he submitted. It was easier than fighting about it all the time. He submitted to Mimi's image of him though it wasn't true.

The writing kept my brother in a constant state of isolation. Days passed when I only saw him at breakfast and dinner. When he wasn't sitting quietly, eyes down, at the kitchen table for meals, Jacob was hidden away in his attic bedroom. He was a phantom, his presence known only through creaking floorboards in the ceiling.

I don't know if Mimi outright told Rebecca and me not to go upstairs, or if the prohibition was something we assumed. But, regardless of the consequences, I couldn't go forever without seeing my brother.

I waited for a weekend afternoon when Mimi was in her basement and I crept up the stairs. I stuck to the edges of the steps themselves so the wood wouldn't whimper under my feet and give me away. By the time I reached Jacob's bedroom door I was sweating like a glass of ice water at a summer picnic. I tapped quietly on the door and turned the iron knob as quietly as I could. My brother was bent over the windowsill, staring at the front yard. It was a dull view, nothing but grass and squirrels, yet he seemed to hold out hope that another kid would come into view, or a car or a bicycle—something to break the monotony. This was Oklahoma Jacob. The fun-loving New Jersey mischief-maker had surrendered and in his place was a flat, sullen boy.

"You okay?" I whispered.

I stayed close to the doorway, so I could hear if anyone was coming up the stairs.

"I hate it here," my brother said.

His right middle finger had a divot on the side of the tip from where the pencil pressed hard against it as he wrote and wrote and wrote. The pencil sitting on the white antique desk was chewed to a nub and rested neatly, eerily, atop a sheet of loose-leaf that was only half filled with today's sentence.

The afternoon heat mixed with the thinly insulated ceiling made this room stale, humid, and heavy. I got a strong whiff of vinegar as the air-conditioning kicked on, rustling the still air to life. I wrinkled my nose.

"What's that smell?"

"I had to pee," Jacob said, unfolding from the sill and opening the closet door. The smell became a stench.

"Mimi yelled at me for being downstairs. She said I was stalling. So I went in here."

I searched my brother's eyes for an indication that he understood how crazy that sounded. But he didn't seem bothered.

We stared into his closet, the scent of the urine-soaked carpet fading away as my nose grew accustomed to it. On the white-washed back wall of the closet, underneath a bookshelf, my brother had written in his now-impeccable cursive, *I HATE MIMI AND GRANDDAD.*

Then, a few weeks after Jacob's eleventh birthday, Rebecca and I were finishing breakfast while Mimi made our lunches at the kitchen counter. We'd been in Oklahoma nearly two years. Jacob passed by Mimi to leave the kitchen and Rebecca looked up at just that moment.

"You're taller than Mimi!" she marveled.

And he was.

By an inch, more if you counted his hair. Rebecca couldn't have known that statement would kick a pebble down the snow-covered mountain of distrust between Mimi and Jacob.

Mimi said, "Soon he'll be eating us out of house and home!" lightly, like it was a joke, but she stiffened her back to inhabit all five feet one inch of her petite frame and I knew that I shouldn't laugh.

Then Mimi started carrying a wooden paint stirring stick with her whenever she was alone with us. She always kept paint stirrers around the house; she used them to mix the gallon buckets of liquid porcelain in her basement workshop, and sometimes to knock boxes off of high shelves. She also found them useful for waggling at our legs to keep us in line. "Don't make me get the spank stick," she'd say, drawing her eyes up to the shelf above the microwave in the kitchen where she kept her largest arsenal. That spot in the kitchen was the North Pole of discipline in the house on Forty-fourth Street. But now Mimi wasn't the only person tall enough to reach her weaponry.

Seeing Mimi wandering the house with a stick in her hand—sometimes two—set my teeth on edge. It made me want to cuss or scream or pitch a fit just to end it, even briefly. But I never craved attention enough to incite a whipping. I buried my face in a book so I wouldn't have to look at the things.

Mimi's sudden fear of my brother was a code I could not crack. I understood his misgivings about her; the solid year and a half of increasingly complicated sentence assignments had calcified a streak of resentment in him.

Neither Mimi nor Granddad had ever raised a boy. Sure, Granddad had been one, but that was so long ago it could hardly be relevant. As far as I could tell, Mimi was afraid of my brother because he was eleven years old and he was bigger than she was. He had spent the past eighteen months of his life being disciplined by her, and he would only get bigger. She could see him every night at the dinner table clenching his jaw rather than talk back, but what if he didn't maintain that self-discipline once he realized he had the upper hand? Mimi was a small lady. I knew what that was like, to go through life with a sense that people and things bigger than you could easily hurt you. I never thought my brother could be one of those things, but Mimi and Granddad had lived so long and seen so much; maybe they knew something I didn't. Maybe because they didn't love my brother like I did they were able to see things in him that I was blind to. It was the only way I could justify the difference between the way they treated me and the way they treated him. And I needed to justify it, because other than my brother fading away from me, I was growing comfortable in Oklahoma.

In Oklahoma from mid-September to the end of October there is a four- to six-week lull between tornado season and ice storm season when the weather takes a break from trying to blot out all human life. After the scorching dog days of August, the early autumn comes in mellow and friendly. It was a day like that when the tension finally broke.

The sunlight shining through gaps in the curtains was bright enough to read by, lending everything a Hollywood-caliber glow. I was alone. I had watched my allotment of television for the day and Granddad was due home from work any minute. I assumed Mimi was in her basement workshop. That's where she always was when she wasn't lying down in her bedroom with a migraine. The sunlight pouring through the dining room window was warm on my belly. Then the rumbling started.

At the top of the stairway the attic door swung open and closed, followed immediately by the squeak of the upstairs bed-room door opening. Then Mimi hollered, "Git downstairs!" her voice pinched and immediate, like air escaping a balloon. Foot-steps stampeded down the stairs. I jumped up from the floor to see Jacob and Rebecca emerge from the staircase, skittish and red-cheeked. I felt my jaw flap open. They had a secret that I was not in on. The realization stung me like a slap.

Mimi was on their heels, herding them to the back of the house with the spank stick.

"You sit there until Granddad gets home," Mimi said to Jacob, pointing the stick at a kitchen chair. She didn't look at Rebecca at all.

Jacob's hair was combed back the way Mimi had shown him how to do when he first moved here. He wore a red-and-brown-striped shirt with a brown collar and cuffs. Jeans. The tough dark kind. His sneakers thunked against the metal legs of the kitchen chair and made a *shoosh* when they brushed the indoor/outdoor carpeting on the kitchen floor. With the flick of her wrist, Mimi cracked the paint stirrer against his calf and he stopped.

My brother slumped in the kitchen chair looking at his empty hands in his lap. Across the vast expanse of hallway, I stood in my bedroom doorway trying madly to catch his eye. The world was crumbling around us. I was afraid. I needed my brother to show me it was going to be okay.

I waved.

Jacob cast a sidelong glance at me but didn't turn. The place was electric with dread, the moment after the roll of thunder when you wait anxiously for the next lightning strike, hoping it will be far, far away.

I turned into the bedroom to find Rebecca hidden in our closet. She crouched on the floor with her eyes wide open, hugging her knees to her chest. She said, "It was just a magazine."

Jacob had gotten his hands on one of Granddad's old *Playboy* magazines. He'd found it in Mimi and Granddad's bedroom closet one day when Mimi was working in the basement. He was looking at it that afternoon when Rebecca trekked upstairs to bring him some cookies she'd liberated from the pantry. She saw the magazine and wanted to look, too.

Maybe if she hadn't been involved Mimi and Granddad would have understood that it was natural for an eleven-year-old boy to be curious about women's bodies. Maybe they would have assigned some sentences about not taking other people's things and left it at that. But now an example needed to be made out of somebody. Outside, Granddad's car sighed into the brick driveway. In the closet where Rebecca and I hid I heard his heavy footfalls advancing down the hall.

Granddad did the same thing every day. He drove forty-five

minutes to the Air Force base, worked eight hours, then drove forty-five minutes back in the afternoon. All he wanted to do when he returned was ride his stationary bicycle and watch the early news in his den. Today Mimi intercepted him. Through the closet door and the double wall that separated my bedroom from the dining room, I heard her tell him that *the boy is a problem* before they walked into their bedroom. I couldn't hear anything more until they walked into the kitchen where Jacob still sat.

In the closet, I synced my breath to Rebecca's. Then I crawled over to the doorway on my stomach. The heavy carpet imprinted itself on my arms and legs. I stretched my head around the doorway just enough to see Granddad's shoulders blocking out my brother, blocking out the light. He was in his suit pants and his undershirt. The outline of his body in the doorway was crisply drawn. He held a belt in his right hand.

I'd heard of belts. When Michael was responsible for us he'd threatened the belt often. And though he never brought one down on me, he reddened the back of my brother's legs a few times over the years. I was lucky to be big-eyed and quiet in those times. But boys were different. They needed to be broken, like horses, with whips and spurs, it seemed.

We are too close, I thought. Too close to the nexus of Granddad's anger and Jacob's badness and Mimi's urging and the vortex those clashing forces created. I knew we were too close because I'd seen anger like this before. I'd seen the look in the eyes of grown-ups cooking up bruises and welts for one another, throwing chairs and plates and all manner of things.

I felt Rebecca's clammy body crawl beside me. In the kitchen Mimi guarded the door to the backyard; Granddad stood between the hallway and the kitchen. Jacob was standing now, his shoulders rolled so drastically that his palms pointed to the wall behind him.

Granddad told Jacob to drop his drawers and my brother didn't argue. He was outnumbered and blocked in. He was an inch taller than Mimi but that didn't matter now. He turned to face the back wall and prepared to bear his punishment.

The last thing I saw was my brother bent over the kitchen chair. I searched the air for my sister's hand and, finding it, pulled her out of our bedroom. I ran to the farthest corner of the house, Rebecca flapping behind me like a cape.

We reached Granddad's den and my legs buckled underneath me. There was no more house; I couldn't run anymore if I tried. I collapsed behind the taupe curtains, next to my sister, so close that I could hear her heartbeat pumping to the same rapid rhythm as mine. I pulled the curtains closed behind us. We were in the light of the setting sun. The plastic backing clacked against our ribs as we sucked in deep breaths of air. Rebecca curled in the corner in a fetal position, her forehead resting on the carpet like she was deep in prayer. I couldn't wrap my arms around her because I needed my hands over my ears to block out my brother's screams from the kitchen. I placed my body over hers, my stomach over my sister's back. There was still something worth preserving in her, some part that didn't know the explosive anger of grown-ups.

Jacob's cries traveled through the air-conditioning vent in the floor. They hit my back like birdshot. I felt my sister's ribs hitting mine; there was not enough air in the room to fill us up.

And then it was silent. The air conditioner cycled on. In its silence the house accused me of not doing anything, of failing to step in, of failing at everything.

Mimi's adult daughter, Jolene, came by the house to visit Saturday afternoon. Jolene was in her mid-forties and thin, with severe black hair and one incisor that had grown in crooked. When Jolene was a little girl Mimi ran a beauty shop. Jolene learned to set and perm hair before she was out of middle school. Mimi had hoped that Jolene would finish college and lead a fascinating, adventurous life. But Jolene left school after two years, when she met and married a Baptist naval officer. Since Mimi's arthritis got bad, Jolene came over once a week to set Mimi's hair in brush rollers. And while the greatest disappointment of Mimi's life might well have been that her daughter didn't go farther into the world than Mimi had herself, she never mentioned it while Jolene had her hands in her hair.

I was tucked around the corner from the kitchen counter where Mimi sat, her hair wet and her shoulders draped in a towel. I had my nose pointed into a Louisa May Alcott book about a girl who got paralyzed in a sledding accident, but I couldn't help picking up tidbits of the women's conversation. The sound of women talking was one thing that always comforted me. In the kitchen Mimi said to Jolene, *You can't be too careful with boys, especially teenagers.* Jolene, who had two boys of her own, *mm-hmm*'d with her mouth full of curler pins and carried on rolling Mimi's hair.

I have the girls to think about, Mimi said. *You can't have that sort of thing in a house with young girls.* Her tone was a lean mixed with a whisper, the same tone I'd heard the Mothers of Marigold Court use hundreds of times when they knew children were around and didn't want us to know they were talking about *sex*.

My guess is, Mimi thought somehow we had inherited the appetites of Peggy and Michael. Their having so many children suggested a criminal lack of self-control, and because of his relation to them, my brother's adolescence could not be allowed to develop without strict guidelines, otherwise it would lead to something grotesque, something strange. *That kind of thing* must be stamped out by force if necessary.

A week later, we took Jacob to the Will Rogers World Airport. He was going back to New Jersey, where he would live with our father. According to Peggy, Michael was the only person Granddad would release custody to. She would always maintain that when she called to protest that Granddad had told her he'd *be damned if that man doesn't raise a single one of his children.*

On the day my brother left Oklahoma, we all walked with him to the airport departure gate. I didn't hold his hand or hug his neck, not with Mimi and Granddad watching so close, not with the image of the belt still in my mind. My brother stepped into the tunnel to the airplane and I watched his blue backpack bob until he reached a bend. He turned and waved. All I could do was stand there while my brother receded.

That night when everyone was asleep, I walked into the kitchen. Moonlight shone through the lace curtains. The table was set for breakfast, cereal bowls turned upside down over the juice glasses like Mimi did each night before bed. The fruit basket in the center was full of bananas. There was always a surplus of bananas because Granddad ate one every morning for breakfast. Before devouring it he made the banana talk to us in a high-pitched mouse voice as if we were unable to distinguish between a magical animate banana and a grown man jiggling the thing around like a puppet. He didn't even try to keep his lips from moving.

I climbed on a kitchen chair and grabbed one. It was oily and cool in my hand. Beneath the firm peel I felt the possibility of softness. So I squeezed. I squeezed its thick yellow skin as hard as

I could. I squeezed with both hands. I wanted to strangle the life, the color, all the bright blandness out of that wretched fruit. But when I let it go, my hands didn't even leave a mark on the flesh; the banana I chose was not yet ripe. Euphoria washed over me nonetheless, a warm wave of satisfaction that came from hurting something and getting away with it.

At breakfast the next morning Granddad reached for that strangled banana. When he peeled it, the fruit inside was brown, goopy like baby food. A powerful surge ran through me—I had ruined something of his and was eager to see how he liked it. I waited for the roaring monster to return, for the belt to come off. I braced myself to take my lashes like my brother had. But the look on Granddad's face was confused, childlike.

As I watched this barrel-chested man holding a squashed banana, my stomach fell into my shoes. I couldn't even say I was sorry; an apology would let him know that I had done it. I knew, deep down, that my badness was nothing close to the adult transgressions I had witnessed, but it landed on me with force because it was mine. And I was ashamed of all of us, ashamed of myself and Rebecca, ashamed of Mimi, and of Granddad; every single last one of us.

Things You Can Tell
Just by Looking

After my brother left, I learned what restraint looked like. When Rebecca and I fussed about who was actually kicking whom under the dinner table, or brought home tests from school with low enough scores that they required a parent's signature, Granddad went silent and looked deep into the empty air to avoid our eyes. When I babbled about how long it might be before Mom could bring us back to New Jersey, Granddad settled firmly into his chair, as if to cement his body to it. As if to keep him from doing something we would all regret. There was something chilling in these gestures. I had seen a monster that day in the kitchen before my brother went away, but Granddad had been the monster. It was possible that he could become that monster again. He knew it as well as the rest of us did.

One night, I was washing dishes in the kitchen when Mimi sat at the table in the corner working on a bit of sewing. I asked her, "What if I went back? Like Jacob?"

Every time I washed dishes after supper, I thought how I hadn't had to wash dishes in Jersey. I thought about how nobody said *supper* in New Jersey. Nobody called soda *pop*. There were beaches and pizza slices and in New Jersey my mom let me fold my slice in half around my finger so the cheese melted together and the grease dripped down my elbow. She did not make me cut it into bite-sized pieces like a baby. Real rock stars like Bruce Springsteen and Bon Jovi came from New Jersey, not a bunch of sappy hillbillies singing about guns and dogs and trucks. I listened to rock music in New Jersey, not the bland oldies and standards that Mimi and Granddad played in Oklahoma. Everything was better in New Jersey. More than all of that, of course, I missed my mother and brother. I kept my face to the wall, kept the water running. It rushed over my hands, loud as a waterfall, and I thought for a moment that Mimi hadn't heard me. "What if I want to go live with my mom?" I said again, louder this time. I wanted to put those words out in the world, see what happened to them.

"Peggy isn't ready for that," Mimi said. I didn't need to turn around to know that she still had her eyes on her hands. She was working with taffeta, so the fabric rustled like bees' wings under her fingers as she moved along the hem. "She might never be ready."

My heart clamped down on the love I had for my mother, like a pit bull on an intruder. I couldn't believe that she *wouldn't* or *couldn't* or *might never*. I knew her differently than Mimi did. I would not give up on her. I locked my knees and pursed my lips at the sink. My mom was going to find a way to bring me back home.

The taffeta stopped rustling behind me. "New Jersey isn't as great as you remember it," Mimi said. She crossed the kitchen and took my chin in her papery fingers, turning my head to look her square in the eyes.

"Your parents often did not take good care of you," she said.

She searched my eyes for comprehension, agreement. I wouldn't give it. Mimi removed her hands from my face and took a breath.

"Do you remember when I came to visit, when you were little?"

I shook my head.

"You were five, maybe six," she said. "Something was . . . funny about you then. So I took you to a doctor. She said someone hurt you. Down. There." Mimi raised an eyebrow. There was a burnt look in her eyes, like this morsel of a story scalded her somehow.

I did remember her visit, vaguely. It was the time Mimi and Granddad drove from Oklahoma to Florida to take Rebecca to Disney World. The time I was so gutted by the fact that some-one was going to the Magic Kingdom and I wasn't that I tried to forget all about it. But Mimi's expression in the kitchen tonight and her tone brushed against a memory that I had buried deeper than that. Something I'd never told anyone.

Years ago, the boy who put on his leg braces just to kick people in Marigold Court had a fort. It was three sheets strung between a dumpster and a wooden fence that separated our ter-ritory from the property of another apartment building around the corner. You would never notice it if you weren't looking for it. The dumpster and the fence made up two walls, the sheets made the other two walls and the roof. The black asphalt floor was covered alternately with brown pine needles and bottle caps. Alongside the fence was a crumbling concrete parking bumper that was the only furniture in the place. An enormous honey-suckle bush grew over the fence from the backyard on the other side. It brushed against the roof of the fort, dropping leaves and flowers when the wind shook its branches. The roof sagged in the middle, heavy with floral debris.

I'd never told anyone how one summer afternoon I happened upon the fort. When he saw my shadow outside, the kid drew the sheet back and said, *Come in.*

It was hot outside, one of those days when the sun hit the pavement and beat back up at you, frying you twice, but inside the fort was shady on account of the shelter of the honeysuckle. The bush took the biggest beating from the heat, making the inside of the fort five degrees cooler than the outside. I sat on the asphalt and he sat on the parking bumper. He held a stick in his right hand like a scepter. It swayed over his head and jostled the roof, sending flowers and leaves into alternating splinters of orange and green where the sun shone through. I was watching the flowers on the roof, thinking how it was like being inside a kaleidoscope, when I felt a sharp, sudden pain in my left shoulder, a force that rocked me back. My elbows scraped along the rough pavement and I saw him drawing the pointed end of the stick back to hit me again.

In the same millisecond, we both realize that a second blow would be redundant; I was already on my back. Then he was on me, his knees on either side of my waist, the stick still in his hand.

He said, *Stay down.* He said, *Lay still,* or he'd have to cut me. He indicated the knife in his belt, a curved and sinister-looking thing that one of his mother's recent boyfriends had bribed him with. There was a glint in his eyes like the bright shard you see when sunlight hits a mirror and pierces you deep into your brain.

Pine needles and pebbles and bottle caps pressed into my back through my cotton dress. He pulled up my skirt and rooted around in my underwear as if searching for loose change.

I was five years old. I hadn't even thought about my body beneath my clothing, but I knew this was bad. I knew because they told us in school on a constant loop to *keep your hands to yourselves* and *keep private parts private*, but those statements got drowned out in the static of the many things grown-ups said that never had any consequences, like *eat your vegetables*, *go play outside*, and *your face is gonna freeze that way*.

My mind could only accommodate the idea that this boy was not keeping his hands to himself and it was somehow my fault. His fingers found a spot inside me and it felt like he was reaching straight into my throat, yanking my tongue down to the floor of my mouth so I couldn't cry out, no matter how much I wanted to. In the years to come, when I heard other kids whispering about *popped cherries* I returned to this moment and I knew that this was when mine was lost. I didn't know what it was, didn't know I'd had it, before someone took it from me.

All I could do was look at the honeysuckle shadows on the roof of the fort and wait for it to be over. I locked my mind away, separated it from my body somehow. It was like this whole thing was happening to some other girl while I was looking at sunlight shining through the flowers. Then I heard the sound of other kids running in the lot.

The wind created by their racing bodies pressed in on the flimsy walls of the fort. The kid perked his ears up, gauged how close they were. He pulled my panties up, wiped his hand on his shorts, and leaned his face so close to mine that I could feel his teeth on my cheek, and he said, "You tell anybody and I'll stick a knife up your pussy."

I don't know how Mimi or a doctor could find that mark on me. I don't know what the doctor would have looked for, or asked, or what the doctor might have seen.

I didn't know how long I had been standing at the sink, staring into the middle space between Mimi and me. She hadn't said a word since *down there*, and I know for certain that I'd been mute, but for how long? I let out a breath that I'd been holding this whole time and Mimi said, "Maybe you don't remember. The doctor said you mightn't," then she turned back to the kitchen table.

"No," I said to her back, "I remember."

I didn't need to say anything else. We both knew that her point had been made.

She knew that my scrubbed-clean memory of New Jersey was bullshit. She'd always known it. Years before she came for us, she knew. She knew it when she let Rebecca go back to New Jersey with my mom. She knew it when she stayed with us for three weeks, negotiating for my parents to turn over guardianship. She knew that it wasn't all games of kick-the-can in the twilight and sitting under linoleum tables listening to women bicker. It was dangerous, dirty, we were hungry most of the time, and around every corner were boys with knives, and broken glass.

I was horrified that Mimi knew this thing about me. Horrified that this bad thing had left such a mark on me that people could tell it just by looking. I wouldn't be going back, not even if I could.

TWO WEEKS later Mimi and Granddad perched themselves on the armchairs in the living room and called Rebecca and me to sit on the couch. We only used this room for company, or Christmas morning when we opened presents. Whatever they had to say was big.

"We've been talking to your mother about adopting you. The two of you," Granddad said.

His words were still hanging in the space between his chair and the sofa when Rebecca leapt up from her seat as if she were spring-loaded. She squealed and wrapped her arms around Mimi and Granddad's necks simultaneously. I couldn't move.

"You don't have to decide right away," Mimi said, but it was obvious that my sister had already decided.

Granddad cleared his throat and looked at me. "You can stay here with us even if you don't want to be adopted."

"You'll get to change your name if you want to," Mimi said. "A whole new start."

Granddad added that if I really wanted to go back to New Jersey, then I could do that, too. It was my choice.

"If I get adopted and you don't, you're gonna be my niece!" Rebecca said, her blue eyes glistening with the same genius as they had on the day when she recognized that Jacob had outgrown Mimi.

Since that day in the kitchen with Mimi, I'd been stunned into submission. They knew what the answer would be. I knew that I would never go back home. Maybe I didn't want to. Maybe I only hung on to the idea of New Jersey out of love for my mother, a desire to be on her team, to support the image of events that she had worked so hard to present to her father and stepmother, a need to prove that, for all her shortfalls, my mother was a great mother, that her love could cover any sin or shortcoming. But it didn't. It couldn't. Nothing I did could change the facts that my mother loving me and my loving her were not enough.

Love was a word that confused things. I needed to pull it out of my vocabulary to clearly evaluate my situation. I was angry about the way Mimi and Granddad had treated my brother. It was difficult to reconcile my resentment at losing him with my eagerness to accept the gift they offered: a fresh start, a new name, something like a family.

Weren't these the things I had imagined having when I whispered with Rebecca and Jacob about Oklahoma? Mimi and Granddad had provided all of the material things that I didn't have with my parents. They ran like clockwork, with a precision that they had perfected over many decades of life. There was plenty they could teach me if I was willing to learn—sewing and sculpture, math and music, discipline and domestic skills. Mimi and Granddad were a framework I could plug into; all I had to do was follow their rules. Perhaps the act of signing papers and changing names would be the alchemy we needed to make us a family. In the face of all of those gains, my losses didn't seem so much. If I went to back New Jersey there were no guarantees; my mother and brother didn't live together there, so I would still be short one of them no matter what. In Oklahoma, at least, I had my sister.

On the day of the adoption, I wore a pink plaid dress with lace at the waist and puffed sleeves that Mimi had made for me at Easter. Since our brother had left, Rebecca had become prone to throwing tantrums about simple things; she wouldn't slip into her matching blue dress until after she hollered for a few minutes about how this place could be COMMUNIST sometimes. But she ultimately fell in line. There was a small hope that licked against my rib cage, like a flame against glass, that the adoption would solidify the vagueness inside me, snap me into focus.

We drove to a courthouse, walked into a wood-paneled room, and the adults signed papers. I thought it would be bigger, like something from a movie. That we would go into a proper courtroom and sit behind a large table; that there would be people in the gallery to see us in our coordinating dresses and think, *What lovely little girls, I'd adopt them, too!* But it was just a conference room, barely bigger than the table in it. When I scooted around the side of the table, my skirt brushed the chairs and the wall simultaneously. It was stuffy and everyone's cheeks shone with sweat.

The judge was a redheaded lady with black-rimmed eyeglasses. She signed a stack of papers and nodded when it was finished. *That can't be it*, I thought. Surely this was just the beginning, the red-haired woman was just the gatekeeper. She would lead us into a grander room, where there would be tests and things to prove ownership. There would be spells and incantations and something to transform us all.

But no, everyone shook hands. That *was* it. Then Mimi, Granddad, Rebecca, and I went to the Social Security office. At a Plexiglas window I signed my new name on my old Social Security number in my most elaborate cursive.

Mary Anna King

The whole affair barely took two hours. In less time than it takes to bake a cake, Mary Agnes Taggart Hall was expunged from the human record. She ceased to exist.

I'd hated my full name, the old-timeyness of it, the way saying *Ag-nes* lifted the back of my throat like I was going to cough up a hairball, the way my initials spelled M.A.T.H. But suddenly I wanted it back. I knew Mary Agnes Taggart Hall. I knew where she belonged, what she sounded like, what her favorite color was. I did not know this newly minted Mary Anna King.

After the Social Security office we picked up cheeseburgers

from a drive-through and Rebecca and I ate in the kitchen while Mimi went down to her workshop and Granddad rode his stationary bike in the den.

Sitting in the kitchen in my pink plaid dress, the thing I wanted more than anything was for someone to fight. This morning I'd woken with an image in my heart: my mother arriving at the courthouse, breathless, saying, *Stop stop stop. I can't part with my Mary. You can't have her. I can't live without her.* But she didn't. I thought there was a chance that Michael would come striding up in his work boots and say he'd fixed things, that he was sorry. But he didn't, either. And now in the silent afternoon I realized the desire for a fight was the reason I went through with the adoption in the first place. I wanted there to be such a scene that someone would have to call the cops and let them figure out who belonged to whom. I wanted to know that it couldn't be so easy to lose me.

In the twilight hours before dinner I went upstairs to Jacob's old bedroom. It had been empty for a year. Since Jacob had left, I'd avoided that room like it was a downed electrical line.

I sifted through desk drawers, searching for any scrap of my brother or my mother that might have been left behind. All I could lay my hands on was a tooth-marked pencil in one of the desk drawers.

The warm light faded as I opened the closet door and pushed winter coats aside to see if my brother's writing was still on the wall. It was. And there was more. Beside the *I HATE MIMI AND GRANDDAD* was a drawing of a monster. The monster had rows of teeth in his open mouth. He held screaming bodies— children—in his claws, en route to his gaping maw. It was drawn in No. 2 pencil, and while the drawing was graphic, included scales and blood, it had a textbook quality to it.

It was grotesque, but something about that monster felt kindred. It was a call that echoed something I felt inside. A hunger that wanted to destroy everything, devour everything, to hurt back, to show Everyone, whoever Everyone was. The people in this monster's hands were kicking and screaming; fighting back. Like my brother had. Like my mother had. Not me. I never fought back. Not today, not ever. I didn't that day in the fort at Marigold Court, or the day when I was sent to Oklahoma. I didn't fight anytime my first parents gave one of my four little sisters away, or the day when Mimi and Granddad sent my brother away. I never fought anything.

Maybe I was not a fighter.

As this attic room wrapped its cold arms around me, I applied the tip of the chewed pencil to the closet wall and added to my brother's drawing. I drew a girl inside the monster's mouth, getting chomped on and swallowed up.

A week later I moved into the upstairs bedroom.

Mimi and Granddad bought me a whole set of matching bedroom furniture that I got to pick out. Ensconced in the attic, away from the perfect trio of Mimi-Granddad-Rebecca, I didn't feel like such an outsider. There was a closet full of hate graffiti up here and the sign on the door read PEGGY'S ROOM. This was where I belonged.

It was the last room people lived in before they left the house on Forty-fourth Street for good.

The Debt

The panic attacks started after my adoption. I'd always been a jumpy kid, but as soon as my name changed my jumpiness got jacked up to new heights. When I got nervous now, my limbs went numb or my breath would stop. Sometimes my heart beat so fast that my ribs throbbed from the impact. Some attacks happened at home, some at school. There was never one single trigger that I could identify. I only knew that, whatever the cause, it was inside me and I couldn't escape it.

Mimi and Granddad witnessed a few of my "spells"; ones where I fell to the living room floor, unable to catch my breath until I nearly lost consciousness. They didn't understand them. The simplest explanation was that I was doing this to myself. Getting myself worked up over nothing, Mimi said. They told me to stop being dramatic and get up. Sometimes they had to scream this instruction because during an attack every sound came to me slowly, as if through eight feet of water. My delay in complying was interpreted as obstinacy. I was too old for fits, Granddad would scold. By the time I started eighth grade, I'd grown familiar enough with the symptoms that I could hide in a bathroom or my bedroom when I felt an attack coming on. So long as no one had to see them, they didn't exist. And the problem was solved.

My new parents seemed to constantly approach me with the tepid hand of obligation and the safety of distance. I interpreted this coldness as a lack of affection. It wasn't a hard leap to make. Peggy had sparked like a campfire when I entered a room. She hung on to every word I breathed into the phone when we spoke. She still sent letters, sheets of loose-leaf paper with her large choppy cursive scrawled across multiple lines. Most of them only said, *I love you and miss you, Meems—love Mom*. But she spent twenty-five cents to mail them. It was a modest sum made larger by the fact that she only made $4.25 an hour as a cashier.

I knew Mimi and Granddad were capable of affection; I saw it every day between them and Rebecca. My sister hung by the sink while Granddad shaved every morning and sat on the side of his armchair while he checked our homework every night. Mimi reached for Rebecca's hand when we crossed parking lots and stroked her hair at the dinner table. They were vigilant about any slight change in Rebecca; a sniffle, a sneeze, a high color in her cheeks, and she was tucked on the couch for the day with her favorite movies and an assortment of treats to woo her appetite. Mimi bought special milk for Rebecca's sensitive stomach, cut her sandwiches into triangles instead of squares. They held the memory of the ailing baby they had saved; she would always be that for them.

Mimi and Granddad fed me, clothed me, and drove me to school. The thoughtful things they did—like sending me to piano lessons or leaving notes from the tooth fairy tucked under my pillow—I suspected they only did to maintain a semblance of fairness. We never used the words *father*, *mother*, *daughter* unless we were required to for school forms. They were my parents on paper.

Maybe it was the paper part that made our relationship feel transactional, like a loan from a bank that I would someday need to repay. Because I had needed to be rescued, Mimi and Grand-dad sacrificed their golden years. They never said as much to me, but I could tell when Mimi's doll club friends talked about second honeymoons to Cozumel and fancy new mattresses with his-and-hers controls that my new parents were missing out. The money they should be spending on trips to Hawaii was instead used to buy school shoes and Christmas trees, to pay for piano lessons and choir trips. Each day I stayed, my balance grew larger. I didn't know how I would ever settle such a debt.

I often wondered why they went through with the adop-tion. Was it to assuage their guilt for missing the warning signs with Peggy? Because of what had happened with Jacob? Did they simply want Rebecca to have a playmate? Or had they done it, as Peggy suggested, only because adoption simplified insurance and tax forms? Mimi and Granddad never let me get close enough to find out.

Granddad kept his thoughts to himself—to an unnerving degree. I guessed he always had. When I came across his senior yearbook, his portrait was captioned, "He's a shy guy, so you'll hit some snarls, but you ought to get to know Charles!" He grad-uated from high school in 1952, making him a member of the Silent Generation, a label I encountered in an old *Time* magazine article that was hauntingly apropos. Granddad never had con-versations on which I could eavesdrop and hear his thoughts. He didn't have any hobbies; he didn't like receiving gifts. As far as I could tell, his only friend was Mimi. Most days the sum of our interaction was when Granddad woke me by singing Irving Berlin's "Oh! How I Hate to Get Up in the Morning" and when he checked my homework after dinner. I learned from Peggy that Granddad had six older sisters, all dead. She also told me that Granddad's father had been a boxer, a man whose first question when he arrived home from work was, "Where are the children so I can beat them?" a story that I was never able to confirm or disprove.

When I asked Granddad about his father he only ever told one story, the one about how his parents met at a church picnic in Philadelphia, just after the turn of the century. His parents both attended with different dates, but happened to spread their picnic blankets beside one another. Before the meal was over, my great-grandfather dumped a bowl of potato salad on the other guy's head and Granddad's parents left the luncheon together. I wanted to know more—was the potato salad fiasco a fight or a joke, what happened next, when were his parents married—but Granddad said that was all he knew. He never talked about his sisters or his first wife—my biological grandmother—Joan.

Mimi wasn't any easier to crack. I didn't have anyone to tell me stories about her past, and she refused to answer a straight question. How many times had she been married? How old was she when she left home? When she was a child, what had she wanted to grow up to be? "Why would you want to know a thing like that?" Mimi would respond, or "Nobody likes a gossip," or "None of your business, young lady." Every once in a while she'd accidentally drop a fascinating biographical crumb, like the fact that she learned to shuffle cards from a boy in a quarantine ward when she had scarlet fever. Or that when she was my age she pin-rolled her hair in bed in the dark for school the next day. She'd get the whole set finished in five minutes, she said. Mimi had one older sister and two younger brothers. Her parents were dead, but Rebecca had met them when she was little. When I asked my sister what Mimi's parents were like (hoping for something to wrap my fingers around), she shrugged and said, "Old."

But when I stopped expecting Mimi to be the same kind of mother Peggy was, I could appreciate her strengths as a teacher. She might not have been forthcoming about her biography, but if I asked her about the right way to do something she'd spend the whole afternoon sewing a dress with me. She taught me how to cut my own hair and how to look sharp with nothing but a handful of bobby pins and a tube of lipstick. Mimi had perfected systems for everything from polishing silver to scooping ice cream and hemming pants.

It was easier to learn about my new parents by the objects they kept around the house. Most everything, even photographs, was tucked into shelves and boxes. I had to dig. Mimi called it snooping; I considered it research. Both words were appropriate. I'd wait until Mimi was downstairs in her workshop, then I'd sift through the trunks in the attic and the photo albums in the hallway.

One day, as I dug through the albums, I found a story that Mimi had written. I assumed it was from the early 1960s; it wasn't dated. It was about a soldier coming home from the Korean War; I never learned how it ended. Mimi found me reading it and snatched it out of my hands. "These are my things," she said. Her voice was even and low. "These are my things and don't be going through them, please."

Beside the leather-bound books were fat binders filled with pedigree charts (genealogy was another one of Mimi's hobbies). Between the binders that contained Mimi and Granddad's respective lineages was a thin volume where Mimi had begun to trace Rebecca's family tree. There were marriage licenses and death certificates for the Freidrichs and Hendrickses and Teels in Mimi's family. Fewer for the Kings and Carlsons in Granddad's. Rebecca's chart had some familiar Halls and Eagans but I was not prepared for the pieces that were missing. The charts only went backward, not forward. I was not on any of them. The few photos I found of myself filled two pages in one of Rebecca's baby books.

The truth became more twisted a few months after our adoption when Granddad decided to rejoin the Catholic Church and take Mimi, Rebecca, and me along with him. In the process, he had his marriage to Joan annulled. It was a formality that allowed Granddad and Mimi's marriage to be blessed by the Church, but it also edited my history further.

Annulment meant that, on paper and in the eyes of God, Granddad and Joan had never married. If they had, in fact, never married, Peggy would never have been born. I wouldn't exist. Maybe I was never meant to. All these pieces of paper, pedigree charts, adoption certificates, birth certificates, marriage licenses, and annulment decrees were meant to set the record straight, but for whom? The annulment was the final act; it pruned my family tree at the root. One hundred years from now, if someone were to look for Mary King, the story they'd find would not include the long shadow of my ill grandmother, a ghostly uncle guardian angel, the trill of my singing daddy, the bone-whiteness of my mother's face.

Was I allowed to keep that past, which I had preserved in my mind with cinematic precision? Was I still me without the stories

I'd been telling myself all my life? What did *me* even mean if I removed all the context around that word? I had an overwhelming desire to crawl under the dining room table like I did when I was little; a desire to fade into the wind or disappear into the walls. To let the world erase me like it seemed to want to.

But there was still a loose thread tying me to the world: the long-lost sisters. Years ago, Peggy had told me that, along with securing promises from my sisters' parents that they would teach the girls about God and send them to college, she had made sure that the adoption agreements contained a clause that the girls would be permitted to search for us once they turned eighteen. Their parents had agreed not to hinder their search if the girls wanted to reunite with us. And if my long-lost sisters didn't look for us, Peggy was permitted to contact them after their eighteenth birthdays, too. Either way it happened, these girls could be back in my life someday. Suppose they wanted to find me? Suppose they had questions that no one else could answer?

The first adopted sister, Lisa, was three years younger than me. She was born in March. If my math was right, I should be twenty-one and about a month shy of graduating from college by the time she started her search. I'd probably be graduated by the time she actually located me. The thought of being pursued thrilled me. I wanted to be wanted, to be admired, to feel connected. Reunion with my sisters would undo all the erasing and chopping of my life.

When my sisters came looking, therefore, I wanted to be there. To be a person worth finding, worth keeping. A person who was un-leave-able.

I tried to imagine what my sisters' lives must be like. I envisioned brick houses with lush lawns and swing sets. I wondered if they played music and had freckles. If they were scrawny and dark like me, or stocky and honey-haired like Rebecca. They would grow up to be doctors and lawyers and English teachers.

So I'd have to be at least as good as that. I couldn't simply exist and hope that they would like me. I had to improve myself. I had to make it through the next few years in Oklahoma, and then become who I wanted to be.

As high school approached, it became clear that Granddad planned to send me to St. Margaret's, the same private Catholic school that Peggy had failed out of three times. I didn't want to go. Not because it was the site of my mother's great academic failure so much as it was a big nothing. As far as I could tell, nobody who went there did anything interesting with their lives. And the prospect of adding four years of private school to my debt to Mimi and Granddad was daunting. I would exhaust every outlet possible before I reached that point.

There was a public performing arts high school on the north side of Oklahoma City, and I decided I wanted to go there. I had been born with a voice people liked to hear. It was something that I inherited from Michael, which complicated my appreciation of it, but when parishioners at church started hiring me to sing their wedding and funeral Masses, I knew I could use it for something. I was unable, then, to decide how I felt about any particular thing without researching how other people felt about it first. Even saying that I "felt" a certain way about something seemed flimsy. I preferred to say that I "thought" a thing. Thoughts were much more concrete. Based on the singing gigs I'd been getting, I thought that attending the performing arts high school would let me use my strengths to get into college, to get scholarships, to get out of Oklahoma. I thought that would be my ticket back to the

East Coast, back to Yankee country where my sisters could find me more easily.

When I mentioned the school at dinner one night, Granddad stared into the kitchen table like it was an oracle. "I don't know," he said. My heart flipped in my chest like a goldfish out of water.

"I don't see any harm in her trying," Mimi countered. "If she's not accepted, she'll go to the Catholic school, of course. It doesn't cost anything to try, Charles."

MIMI TOOK me to the audition. I stood in the curve of a baby grand piano and sang "Amazing Grace." My voice bounced around the white-tiled room like it had in the bathroom of Marigold Court all those years ago. The school called a week later to tell me that I had been accepted. Granddad still thought it was impractical, but if Mimi thought the place was good, then he'd allow it.

I was a vocal performance major, which meant mandatory auditions for choirs, ensemble performance groups, and the annual musical. After the first week I was assigned to show choir, women's show choir, advanced chorus, and a supporting role in *Oliver!* It was the first play I had ever done, the first time I was asked to memorize lines without music. I discovered at my first rehearsal that I loved it. When I entered a scene, I had words on my tongue; I was never stuck with nothing to say, never stymied by the possibility that my own words could betray something spurious about me.

I made most of my friends at school by watching their facial expressions, listening to their speech patterns, noting their gestures, and mirroring them back. It wasn't a foolproof strategy;

most people didn't like me when we first met. I was too distant and analytical, pocketing their characteristics for later use. After a couple interactions, though, my new friends would laugh and say, "When I first met you, I thought you were so weird!" but they could never place exactly why they had thought so, or what had made them change their minds.

I wasn't interested in boys, though with the help of the Judy Blume repertoire, I was deft at faking it. My locker partners and lunch mates loved to discuss the hands of the trumpet players in the jazz band or the broad shoulders of the one boy in the dance department, but the thought of a boy, of anyone, touching my body made me break out in a cold sweat.

When Rebecca graduated from middle school she applied to the music program at my school, too. The prevailing wisdom in the house on Forty-fourth Street was that my sister was the more naturally gifted of the two of us—both intellectually and musically—but I was more disciplined. It never occurred to me that Rebecca wouldn't be accepted to the program. A week after her audition, the phone call came. Her class was already full, there were no slots in the music program for more incoming freshman.

She said she didn't care, but I could see there was a new separation between us. Rebecca enrolled in the private school and went on to dominate the music department there. She taught herself to play the guitar and composed heart-bleeding songs about girls who were no good. The creative community in Oklahoma City was small but vibrant. So, though we attended different schools, Rebecca and I frequently crossed paths at coffee shops and open mic nights where the artsy kids from my school and her school intermixed.

On those nights, no one believed we were sisters. Rebecca

wore mud-caked bell-bottom jeans slung low on her hips and cut deep x's between her knuckles with a black ink pen, while I wore sweater sets buttoned all the way up to my neck. My hands jittered from the caffeine in my chai lattes, while my sister smoked cigarettes in the parking lot and enthusiastically sipped soda cans filled with Everclear. All my sister's friends called her "Becca." I was always confused when they talked about Becca's music and Becca's guitar and Becca's grades; the day my sister stamped her foot in New Jersey and insisted that her *name* was *Rebecca* was so powerfully etched in my memory that I'd forget she'd changed it. When I did remember and said, "Oh, you mean *Rebecca*!" her friends would roll their eyes and my sister would say, "You see what I'm dealing with?"

It was the mid-nineties, the rebirth of female singer-songwriters and the creation of Lilith Fair. My Julie Andrews–style soprano lacked the personality that an open mic rewarded, but my sister's husky alto voice was right on trend. She crooned in ripped jeans while older hippie types hung around the bathrooms telling girls they sounded like Janis Joplin. I couldn't tell Rebecca that her duct-taped guitar, the patchouli oil she wore, the smell of weed and day-old whiskey sweating through people's pores sent me back to the rooms full of sad men saying, *Gimme me a kiss, gimme a kiss*. She wouldn't know what I was talking about or, worse, she might think it sounded romantic in its realness and be inspired that the life of a troubadour burnout was in her blood. So on those open mic occasions I stayed out of the spotlight, clapping politely at others' performances, until I could hitch a ride home with someone with a car who was ready to leave.

Rebecca and I could have bought a car to share if I was willing to combine my earnings from a part-time job at the Gap with her wages from the Sears juniors department, but I was saving everything for my future life. It was one of the many ways I disappointed her. I also refused to break down any barriers that Granddad erected to dating or curfews. She insisted that as the oldest it was my job to press the boundaries so our parents would be more lenient with her, but the thought of willingly provoking a disagreement with Mimi and Granddad was out of the question. I was resigned to the notion that I owed Mimi and Granddad not only for my life, but also for the life of my sister. With all her sneaking out of the house and the cigarettes she smoked behind the garage, Rebecca wasn't doing anything to pay down our balance herself. I threw away the empty vodka bottles I found under her nightstand so Mimi and Granddad wouldn't find them and have a heart attack.

By the middle of my high school career the prospect of solitude horrified me. When I was alone, a deep sucking sense of darkness overcame me. If I gave in to it, I feared I would never find a way out. It wasn't the physical sensation of being alone so much as the way my thoughts ran when no one else was around. That was the reason I never experimented with drugs and booze like Rebecca. I couldn't be out of control—I wasn't sure what would come out if I let my guard down. I wasn't sure how to behave without other people around me to mirror. It seemed that all my biggest errors were made when I was left to my own devices.

Early one evening during my senior year of high school, I happened to be near the phone when it rang. The voice on the other end of the line asked for Becca, and instinctually I said that they had the wrong number; no one named Becca lived here. As soon as the phone clicked into the receiver, my sister bounded around the corner and I remembered. I knew how important a name could be to a person; my name was certainly important to me. My sister had asked me hundreds of times to call her Becca, especially around her friends. My failure to do so reeked of contempt. I braced myself for one of her usual stomping and screaming fits, but it didn't come.

"I tell you things and it's like you're not even here," she said.

She was right. I wasn't there. I was far, far away: from her; from Forty-fourth Street; from Mimi and Granddad; from Oklahoma.

I'd been gone for a long time.

Wake Up

After I graduated from high school, I had a summer job at a nationwide call center where I booked rental cars for people in exotic locales like Danbury, Connecticut, and Jackson Hole, Wyoming. I still refused to spend any money on a car myself, but Granddad had retired by then and didn't seem to mind giving me a ride when I needed one.

One afternoon two weeks after my high school graduation we were in the Chrysler, a new gold one that he'd bought himself as a retirement present. He kept his eyes on the traffic on the Lake Hefner Parkway, his hands locked at ten-and-two, when he told me, "Mimi's sick."

"Is it cancer?" I asked. She'd had a bout with breast cancer during my junior year of high school. They found it early and performed a mastectomy—she had been fine since then. But I knew that cancer could come back. It always did in the movies.

"It's not cancer," Granddad said. "They think it's kidney failure." A membrane of water clung to his blue eyes. He didn't look at me and he didn't blink.

Whenever we had reason to discuss Mimi's health over the years, Granddad always said, "Don't you worry, Mimi-Mouse is going to outlive me. By a *long* shot," and he'd point out that Mimi's parents had lived into their nineties. Granddad talked that way through every one of Mimi's migraines, asthma attacks, and the increasing number of pills she took with her breakfast. He said it through the breast cancer and the mastectomy. But he did not say it today.

Mimi would need to start dialysis treatments as soon as possible. She was going into surgery the next day to insert a tube in her stomach. Then, once a week doctors would connect her body to a machine to clean her blood. The only other option was a kidney transplant. But new kidneys went to twenty-year-old diabetics or kids with rare congenital diseases, not seventy-four-year-old women who had recently had cancer.

"It'll be a simple procedure," Granddad said. "She'll be home before you are tomorrow."

But when I finished work the next day, Becca was waiting for me in the parking lot. She sat on the back bumper of the old gray Chrysler chewing her cuticles. This was strange: Granddad hadn't sold the old car yet, but he never let Becca or me drive it. Not unless it was an emergency.

"Mimi's not waking up," my sister said.

Becca and I drove to the hospital. Granddad had asked us to bring a pair of pajamas for Mimi so she wouldn't be cold. Mimi was on the eighth floor, in the intensive care unit. The tile floors, fluorescent lights, and the strange lady behind a desk sent a tremor through my psychic landscape.

"We're here to see Mrs. King," Becca said.

"There are no visitors in ICU, I'm sorry, girls," The woman behind the desk said.

"We're not visitors," I said. "We're her daughters." I tilted my head to indicate the bundle of clothes in my hands. Who but daughters would bring pajamas, slippers, and a toothbrush?

The woman squinted her eyes at us; she must have been thinking about seventy-four-year-old Mimi, frail and curled and unconscious in a hospital bed on this floor, wondering how it was possible that woman had daughters our age. She was suspicious.

"We're adopted," I said, and she waved us through.

The hallway breathed with machine sounds, whirrs and clicks surrounded us as we passed dark rooms.

The blue-white spotlight above her bed was the only light source in Mimi's room. Her eyes were open but unfocused, and her hands wandered slowly across the nubby white blanket that was tucked snugly around her chest and under her arms.

"She's awake," Granddad announced as we walked through the door. Becca stood at the edge of the light pool, her arms hugging her waist as if she needed them to hold her organs inside. A doctor entered the room carrying X-ray films. They rumbled like thunder as they curled in his hands.

He was a pulmonologist, one of a team of specialists—also including a cardiologist, gerontologist, and pathologist—whom Mimi's original doctor had consulted when she didn't wake up after her surgery. The pulmonologist showed us two X-rays of Mimi's lungs: one that he had taken that morning, and one that Mimi's oncologist had taken two years ago, after she'd had her mastectomy.

"See this scar tissue here?" he said, pointing to the two X-rays. The recent one looked decidedly more cobwebbed.

It had never been her kidneys. It was there in black-and-white. Mimi's kidneys were fine—well, not exactly *fine*, but they weren't what was killing her. The general anesthesia for the surgery this morning had caused her oxygen level to plummet, and because her lung capacity was so decreased with all that scarring—"fibrous tissue," the doctor kept correcting himself— she couldn't get enough oxygen with each breath. That effect had snowballed to the rest of her body.

"It is called pulmonary fibrosis," he said. He told us that they weren't sure what had caused it. Possibly the chemicals Mimi had inhaled over the twenty years she ran her beauty shop, or maybe she aspirated a bit of porcelain dust in her doll-making workshop.

"The only cure is a lung transplant," the doctor continued.

If Mimi had been least likely to get a new kidney, she would never get a set of lungs. "She probably has about five years left on the lungs she's got," the doctor continued.

Right now the hospital would focus on getting Mimi's body re-oxygenated. Her muscles, organs, and brain were operating on a trickle of the oxygen that they required. She would need physical therapy, breathing treatments, steroids. Mimi would be here for a while.

Granddad spent every day at the hospital, arriving there in the morning after he dropped me off at work. When he picked me up in the afternoon, we bought an extra-large milkshake for Mimi—the serious kind made with two scoops of ice cream— because Mimi didn't like the hospital foods. She was losing weight, but she needed calories if she was going to get better.

I was shocked by how quickly Mimi's body deteriorated. After a couple of weeks her calf muscles and forearm flesh dangled off her bones like flags. She rarely made sense when she spoke, but the nurses assured me that she was "making progress."

I rarely saw my sister in those days. Becca slept late every morn- ing, and when I got home at night she was jamming with her band or passed out in her bed with her jeans still on. The most time I spent with her was on Sunday mornings when Becca, Granddad, and I attended Sunday Mass, our weekly performance of family unity.

My sister failed to understand something that I thought was self-evident: in the face of illness, the family was meant to suffer, too. Their suffering was part of the cure. If sunny days were left to ripen and rot on the vine, if rosary beads were clicked together in urgent calypso-like rhythm, if fewer hours were slept, more coffee consumed—consumed, not enjoyed, in trough-sized amounts that gave me stomach cramps when I stood up—that would somehow protect Mimi.

Mimi's daughter Jolene understood this. Every day that I spent in the hospital with Mimi, I saw Jolene's handiwork. She curled and styled Mimi's hair, perched hypoallergenic plants on the windowsill, and rolled new socks with skid-resistant grippers on Mimi's feet. I wondered if Jolene saw my offerings when she was there. Did she notice the expanding collection of unscented lotions on the nightstand? Could she tell that I had rubbed those emollients into Mimi's papery skin on her arms and legs, massaged her floppy muscles to increase blood flow? Had Jolene noted that Mimi's fingernails were filed in ovals and her toenails clipped? Had she seen the thick novel whose bookmark was moving steadily through its pages as I read aloud to Mimi each day?

I introduced myself over and over. I'm her daughter, I said, so the day nurses would tell me Mimi's current oxygen level. I told physical therapists, "She's my mother," when they chirped about how glad Mimi must be to have such a devoted granddaughter. I used the word *daughter* more in the hospital that summer than I had in the seven years prior.

As the weeks became months, Mimi grew more cognizant, though still physically weak. Walking to the bathroom required assistance and even with someone to lean on she got winded after more than five steps. She needed to exercise to revive her muscles, but exercise exhausted her. Then she needed to nap. Sometimes in a half-awake state she'd turn to me with empty cupped hands and say, "Take this kitten away, would you, it's too hot." And I would be unsure if she was awake or asleep; if I should humor her or point out that there was no cat. Maybe forcing her to stare at that fact would lead her out of her confusion. Maybe that was precisely what she needed, my refusal to wander into her dreamworld with her. I would look over my shoulders for a health care professional to offer guidance. When I didn't see one I would scoop the phantom cat from Mimi's hands and pretend to tuck it underneath my chair.

I was supposed to leave in three weeks to attend college in central New York. It was arranged before Mimi got sick, but I was no longer sure that leaving was the right choice. It occurred to me that there was a silver lining here if I was willing to take advantage of it. In Mimi's illness was a way that I could finally repay Mimi and Granddad for the years of their lives that they spent raising me; I would reimburse their time with my time. I could stay. If I enrolled in the University of Oklahoma I could remain in the house on Forty-fourth Street and do whatever was needed.

I could have enrolled in OU without telling them. I could have simply done it. But some part of me still needed another person to approve my plan so I would know it was good.

My opportunity came on a mid-July afternoon after Mimi's daily dose of *Murder, She Wrote* reruns. By late July she was having more good days. She could carry on conversations without losing her train of thought midsentence. She could make and hold eye contact. Her doctor had predicted that she had five more years, but forecasts could be wrong. I couldn't be sure that I'd have another opportunity to say what I needed to say.

The way I felt about her was the echo of something I remembered feeling a very long time ago with my first mother, when I was a different person. My love for my first mother was sometimes, I thought, too intense. It warped me, that much closeness. It scooped a divot deep in my soul that would never be properly filled. Mimi and I would never have that sort of connection. The two-foot gap between my chair and her hospital bed that afternoon was physically the closest we had ever been.

"I'm sorry for all the trouble I caused you," I said, giving Mimi the opportunity to say that I was no trouble, that she was glad to have someone to teach all the things she knew, an empty vessel for her to pour her knowledge into, such an eager pupil.

She said, "I know. I already know."

"It's not too late for me to stay," I continued with my second line, looking at her knees shifting under the nubby blanket.

I mentioned that the state university accepted applications until the end of July. I could stay in the house on Forty-fourth Street, keep it in order until she was better. I could take care of her because she had taken care of me.

"No, no. You can't stay . . ." she said, shaking her head, closing her eyes with the effort. "You have to go." She reached for my hand. Her fingers were the lightest I had ever felt them. "You can come back and tell me all about it."

She started to cough then, and the respiratory therapists arrived to administer her breathing treatment. I walked laps around the hallway to warm myself until they were done, thinking about what had just happened.

On the day of my adoption, I had looked for a grand gesture to show that someone cared about having me or losing me. But when I performed such a gesture for Mimi, for the woman I had been telling people was my mother all summer, she refused it. I wanted to be relieved—I should have been relieved—she had let me off the hook. I wouldn't have to be a seventeen-year-old nurse. I could to go college, and parties, and be whoever I wanted to be. But this crossroads was ominously familiar. I couldn't consider this present situation without thinking about the choice I'd made when I left Peggy. Here I was, years later, abandoning another mother at the lowest point in her life in pursuit of something better, something for myself. I regretted leaving Peggy every day, and I knew that this departure would trouble me the same way. A truth pulsed in my mind like a neon sign: Daughters stayed. In every story about family and illness I had encountered—from *Little Women* to *What's Eating Gilbert Grape*—family stayed close. But maybe I had overlooked something. Maybe in those stories the characters stayed close because they were held close. And I wasn't.

Mimi was released from the hospital a week before I left for New York. She had more accessories now, an oxygen machine that sat in the living room with hundreds of feet of hollow tubing that tethered her to it, a wheelchair, a walker, a traveling oxygen tank, and enough bottles of pills to fill half a kitchen cupboard. Granddad portioned the pills into a container with twenty-eight compartments and wrote detailed notes for Becca to administer them over the next four days, when Granddad would be driving me to New York.

Granddad and I packed the new Chrysler early on an August morning. The sky was still dark when I slid the last plastic bin in the backseat. Becca shuffled to the front door and leaned out, barefoot and pajama'd, to watch me. Her hair hung in her face like a beagle's ears.

"I'm going to miss you," she said.

Her arms were crossed and I could see a fresh *x* cut deep in the flesh between her right-hand thumb and index finger. I tucked her hair behind her ears, folded her in my arms, and hugged her tight. She was still two inches taller than I was—she always had been—but she suddenly seemed small.

"Keep Mimi out of the liquor cabinet," I croaked into her ear.

She rolled her eyes and let me go.

It was hard for me to believe that I was leaving Oklahoma. I had planned it for so long. But I'd spent most of that time thinking about the obstacles that would have prevented my success. I had arranged reactions, ways to circumnavigate, options A through F. I'd imagined my exit millions of times. But now that my plan was falling into place I found it impossible to relish the moment. New struggles reverberated in my mind, millions of things that could still derail me.

I wouldn't know anybody. There would be no one around to define who I was in relation to them—Granddad's and Mimi's daughter, Becca's sister—no one would know anything about me unless I told them.

I HAD two days to figure out what I would say.

PART THREE

found

2000–2011

Hammered

When Granddad and I arrived at my college in central New York, I was three weeks past my eighteenth birthday, painfully virginal, reeling from Mimi's illness, and fragile as a hothouse orchid (though I would sooner die than admit any of these things to another living soul). When we parked on the campus, a golf cart full of neon-shirted upperclassmen chirped that all we had to do was unload my boxes from our car and they would cart them up "the Hill" for me. Once we were stripped of the business of the moving my boxes from car to dormitory, Granddad's presence seemed unnecessary.

"Well . . ." he said, "I could just get back on the road. Unless you want me to stay?"

He would stay if I asked, but Mimi and Becca needed him in Oklahoma more than I needed him here; we both knew it was true. I told him I'd be fine.

Whoever set the agenda on move-in day knew what he was doing—walking up the Hill from the field in front of the Hall of Presidents was the most picturesque way to see the campus. The buildings draped down a hillside where the Adirondack Mountains melted into the Chenango Valley. I chewed on those words *Adirondack*, *Chenango*, as I hiked up the hill. Butter-yellow daffodils grew in profusion around the dark lake at the main entrance. Every wend in my path revealed green lawns soft as mink, benches tucked in niches, tree roots arranged like cups inviting reflection and repose. Vines grew up the base of the older limestone buildings; it was Camelot-like. Precisely what I was looking for when I picked this place from the piles of catalogs in my high school guidance counselor's office.

The nearest airport was an hour away and the nearest train was thirty minutes. The remoteness was the most appealing aspect. This college was a fortress between me and the chaotic forces of the rest of my life.

No one noticed me as I made my way up the path; they were absorbed in their own dramas. I sensed who belonged to whom from the invisible pulses between this outstretched hand and that arched eyebrow, this hand in that hair, along that shoulder. The Esperanto of connection, a language that I only ever learned well enough to read but not speak.

Lonesomeness clawed in my sternum. I didn't wish Granddad had stayed or that I had Michael in his place. It wasn't about Mimi or Peggy, either. I wanted something I'd never had. The thing these other people had: a clear, obvious connection with a parent. Someone who not only provided for my care and feeding, but lit up like a Christmas tree when I walked into the room, who had to clutch their heart when I left. I envied these families on the quad who took that sort of thing for granted.

I shook my head and reminded myself that the last eight years of my life had been about preparing for this. Not for college per se, but for the family that college would help ready me for. I'd buried myself in schoolwork, test preparation, music clubs, and after-school jobs to buy myself the luxury of four years to become a person worth finding.

My boxes were waiting for me in my dorm room when I arrived, as were my roommates. I'd lucked into a spot in a two-bedroom suite. I was to share the front room with a pink-haired Long Islander named Sadie. Our wide double window looked onto the academic quad. The sill wasn't wide enough to be a true window seat but I tucked myself on it anyway, stuffing the corners with pillows and blankets to smooth the edges. Many nights around sunset I would dangle my bare legs out the unscreened window and tease the chilled, empty air with the thought that I could jump out. It made Sadie uneasy. "You can open the window from the top, you know," she'd remind me, and I'd pretend not to hear her.

Sadie and I both came from Catholic households, were studious nerds in high school, and it was clear from the lack of labels on our clothing and the speed with which we secured on-campus jobs that we were both scholarship kids. The previous June, when the Department of Residential Life mailed letters with the names and phone numbers of our future roommates to all of us, Sadie called me first. We had a polite conversation where she advised me not to cut my hair short as I was planning, because I'd want it to cover my ears in the winter. She was a sensitive, sensible girl who dressed almost exclusively in black: the East Coast version of the creative types I knew from my artsy high school. But I didn't come halfway across the country to be the person I had been before. I wanted new everything.

A San Franciscan named Abigail and a recent Russian immigrant named Elena occupied the adjoining back bedroom. Like Sadie and me, Abigail and Elena shared a lot of biographical bullet points with one another: They were pretty girls who knew they were pretty and were accustomed to being rewarded for it. Boys smiled at them in the dining hall and turned to watch them walk away. Their mailboxes filled regularly with delicacies from home—pastries from Abigail's favorite San Francisco bakery, snuggly woolen things from Elena's people, who had settled in Alaska. Both played sports in high school, and in college they jogged daily with obsessive urgency. They disliked one another with an intensity that is usually reserved for one's own reflection.

The second week of school, at nine o'clock on a Tuesday night; my roommates and I were already in our pajamas. Elena made herself a bowl of herbal tea, filling the room with the smell of honey and warm milk. Under the strains of the Abigail's computer playing the Dave Matthews Band, we were all tapping out the first five-hundred-word essays of our undergraduate careers when the phone rang.

Sadie answered it, saying, "Hello?" then, "Hold on." She stretched the phone toward me and announced, "It's for you."

My pulse thrummed in my arms. It had to be Mimi. *Mimi's dead. Mimi's dead and I am not there and I should have stayed and I didn't.* I focused on keeping my hand from shaking as I took the phone from Sadie.

"Hello?"

"Is this Mary King?" a strange boy's voice asked on the other end.

"Um, yeah, speaking . . ." I stammered.

"You don't sound like you're from Oklahoma . . ." he said, his voice heavy with the suspicion that this early in the conversation I was already duping him.

"Who is this?" I demanded.

"This is Blake, from the Beta House," he answered. "We'd like to invite you down for a little party tonight."

No boy had ever called me out of the blue in my entire eighteen-year life. I rifled through the library of my mind, frantically searching for the right way to behave in this situation. I'd never seen someone else have a conversation like this up close. And I'd already snapped at him. Oh god. Oh god, oh god, oh god, he was waiting for me to say something.

"Tonight?" I said.

"Around ten, ten-thirty."

"Um . . . I've got an early class tomorrow, so—"

My roommates circled for crumbs of the conversation.

"Bring your roommate if you want to . . ."

"I've got three."

"The more, the merrier!"

"I'll check with them, but we're all in our pajamas already."

I'd read somewhere that a lady never accepted a last-minute invitation. A lady probably never volunteered information about pajamas, either. God, I was mangling this.

Blake paused.

"We really hope you make it down. We'd love to meet all of you."

"Thanks for the invitation," I said and hung up.

When I relayed the other side of the conversation to my roommates, Abigail groaned into her hands.

"You just told the Betas that we're in our pajamas. At nine o'clock!"

"What's a Beta?"

"It's a frat! They just invited you to a *party* and you told them that we're in our *pajamas*."

"You can go if you want to."

"They invited *you* . . ."

"If you want to go, I'll go."

"Nah . . ." Abigail exhaled heavily. "I mean, I'm already . . . you know. In my pajamas."

The craving for something to erase the taste of that phone call overwhelmed me. I wanted to tap my face against the tile bathroom wall until the words he'd said and the ones I'd said back stopped echoing in my skull, but there were too many eyes; I couldn't do it. They'd report me to Psych Services. The only choice was to sit at my desk and act like that was exactly how I meant to play it. Like I got invited to parties so often that I couldn't be bothered. Like I was not that very minute wondering how the boy on the other end of the line obtained my name and number, why he decided to dial me up, and if that meant that he liked me (if that meant I was likable).

Then Elena looked up from her tea and in her mysterious Russian accent countered, "It is so last-minute. How rude of him." I was so relieved I could have leapt onto her lap.

"I don't know how he even got the number," I said, hoping I sounded blasé.

"From the *Inky*, obviously," Abigail muttered, using the colloquial abbreviation for the *Incunabulum*, a booklet of photographs of every member of our freshman class with their hometown, high school, and dorm room address listed alongside. "The frats go through it looking for cute girls and then they call them up."

This information made me reel. Someone had an idea about who I was. Someone had seen what I looked like and assumed I would know certain things, sound and act and *be* a certain way. Someone thought I was *cute*. I turned my face to the wall to hide the smile creeping across my face. I reached for my copy of the *Inky* in the mess of books on my desk, flipped through until I found my photo. I wanted to see what information this mysterious boy had referenced, curious if I could conjure the same image he had of me and, perhaps, find some way to be that girl in life.

All I was to people here was a smiling black-and-white picture and a short bio: Mary King, Oklahoma City, Oklahoma, East Hall, Room 502. That was all anyone knew about me.

Whole chunks of my life had already flown off me like scrap paper. It was a relief to be rid of the past I'd spent so many years wrestling with. When asked, I told people that I was *born* in New Jersey but *raised* in Oklahoma. That my father was in the Air Force and my mother was a homemaker; that I had one sister. It was easy to be swept away in the bustle of the campus. I joined an a cappella group and a theater club. I read books, wrote papers, and volunteered to play piano at Sunday Mass. I smiled a lot. I tried to project a Plains-state wholesomeness.

ONE DAY another few weeks in, I found myself alone in the suite. I was only five hours away from South Jersey, from Peggy and Michael and Jacob, whom I hadn't seen in seven years. I'd spoken to Peggy on the phone every couple of weeks through high school, Jacob every few months when he happened to be at Peggy's apartment. When the noise of the world stopped I could hear the siren call of their proximity: it latched onto my hand and dragged me toward the phone; it moved my thumb across the keypad. In my ear, the phone rang with the same pitch as the pay phone that rang in Marigold Court all those years ago.

I said, "Hi, Mom," when Peggy picked up the other end of the line.

"Mary!" she squealed. Her pleasure thrilled me. I settled into the conversation like a bird into a nest.

We talked about Jacob. He'd enlisted in the Army and just got back from boot camp. Then about Mimi, whose health was hardly better than when I'd left her.

"You wouldn't recognize her," I said, forgetting for a moment that I was talking about my second mother to my first mother and that might be a cavalier thing to do. Mimi and Peggy still had their own strained stepmother/stepdaughter relationship to deal with, and Peggy still blamed Mimi for the way Jacob was ostracized in Oklahoma all those years ago.

I downshifted to the weather, saying that I forgot how quickly winter comes on the East Coast. Peggy told me that they were already putting out the Thanksgiving items at her store. For the past four years she'd been working as a price-change specialist at a department store. She walked the aisles with a sticker gun and a spreadsheet, working her way through the leftover odds and ends, pricing them to move. She didn't have to deal with people much, which was exactly how she liked it. As she grew older she more frequently said things like, "People are shitty. I don't need more friends." Then she told me that she'd been reading about my school on the Internet.

"Family Weekend's the second weekend in October," she said. "Maybe we'll come up."

I knew Family Weekend was soon and that parents were supposed to visit during that time, but it never occurred to me that the woman I remembered from Marigold Court, the woman who sometimes kept me home from first grade because she was so lonely, could be here.

"I'll get Jacob to drive me," she said.

I could have said don't come, that I wasn't prepared to explain her and Jacob to my friends. Or I could have preserved her feelings with a small lie, said that I needed to catch up in my classes.

But it was clear that she'd made a plan. On a long price-change shift with the sticker gun in her hand she'd imagined writing her name in the red binder in the break room, requesting time off the second weekend in October, and in the column titled "Reason for Request" scribbling, *Family Weekend at Daughter's College.* She had looked up the fastest route to drive from South Jersey to Central New York, found economically priced nearby motel rooms, and decided that it was possible. My doubts were dwarfed by her desire.

And so, of all the things I could have said, "I can't wait to see you!" was what came out of my mouth. It was true, but it complicated my life considerably.

For the next two weeks I dashed to my classes at cheek-reddening pace, wondering how I would explain Peggy to my roommates, who were under the impression that my Mother, my Real Mother, was laid low by a lung disease; I'd had to tell them to explain my suspicious lack of parents on move-in day. My identity was so carefully constructed here; I had been doing so well. All it took was one moment of lonesomeness for me to let my former life invade my new place. My roommates wouldn't understand that there wasn't a lexicon to discuss my family; they would simply think I was a liar and a strange, pathological person. In the days before Peggy and Jacob arrived, I worried the fabric of my story until it fell apart, threadbare, in my mind. Then I gave up and decided to play it by ear.

This would be the first time in eleven years that Peggy, Jacob, and I would be alone together. The prospect was both maddening and exciting.

On the Saturday morning of Family Weekend, they arrived at nine o'clock. Abigail and Sadie were out to breakfast with their families. Elena's people were in Alaska and would have spent more time in airports than on campus if they'd made the trip.

"Who is coming for you?" Elena asked me from the other room.

I flipped through the words that would apply, trying to choose the simplest ones . . . My older sister and my nephew? That was who Peggy and Jacob were on paper, but suppose she encountered them and they said something different. Cousins, maybe? Aunt? It all seemed ridiculous.

"My brother and my mom," I said.

"Is your mom better?" she asked.

"This isn't . . . that mom. This is my birth mom," I said. "I'm adopted." I waited for these words to shatter glass, to tip off an earthquake, but they didn't seem to have any external impact. All their confusing force was turned inward on my gut, as my stomach growled at me in protest.

I left Elena in the suite and headed down to the parking lot to wait for them. The morning was gray and crisp. I sat on a wooden pylon at the edge of the parking lot by the dining hall, watching as my classmates entered and exited with their parents, a crowd of Lilly Pulitzer prints, pleated khaki slacks, boat shoes. I waited until a white sedan with rental placards on the plates turned the corner.

My brother was driving; it was strange to see that he was a grown man now. Peggy leapt from the car while the engine was still running. "Meems!" she hollered. No one had called me that since I was seven years old; it was a name that no one other than Peggy knew. It drew me toward her like iron to a magnet.

Jacob appeared over her shoulder. "It's fuckin' cold here!" he said.

They looked like shadows, Jacob in a black leather jacket and Peggy in a black knee-length coat. Her once-chocolate-brown hair was dyed red, gray roots peeking through at her temples. It fell straight and flat against her cheeks; I couldn't bury my face in her hair anymore.

Over the intervening years since I had left her in New Jersey, I'd carried a picture of her in my mind. Loss had made my image of my mother grow soft and saintly, rendered in watercolor: graceful and strong, her golden eyes wide and calm. In this parking lot, however, the real mother and the imagined one slapped against each other like the simultaneous striking of two adjacent piano keys, their dissonant pitches so close together that they begged to be resolved.

Both faces had the same form: round cheeks and soft chin— the Cupid's-bow lips that I inherited from her—but the Real Peggy's eyes had the scorched look of a person who had been lost at sea. She carried her shoulders high against her ears as if she were constantly braced to receive a blow, and she was smaller than I remembered. When I was seven years old, she towered over me at five feet two inches tall, but now I was two inches taller than her and my arms wrapped all the way around her back. She was still plump and carried most of her weight in her chest. Her breasts had grown a cup size larger with each subsequent pregnancy—I remembered that—but I'd assumed they would deflate once her body realized she didn't have any babies. They hadn't.

How much cleaner it would be if she could have stopped being a mother. A man can walk away and live his life, no one knowing for sure if he is a father, but I understood, looking at Peggy's body which still carried the marks of all of her lost children, that she would always be their mother. Hands that once cradled infants may empty, a body that once curled around another life like a warm shell may grow distant over time, but that body will never be the same. Being a mother had changed her forever.

"I brought you presents!" Peggy said.

Jacob popped the trunk of the car open and grabbed two paper bags the size of suitcases.

"Calm down, Ma," he said. "We got all day to get through."

When we arrived at my dorm room, Elena was draped in my window seat, waiting. Perhaps I had not adequately telegraphed my desire to be unwatched. I made the introductions with my arms flopping like a marionette—Mom, Elena, Elena, Mom, Jacob.

"Here, here, here," Peggy said as she unpacked the bags onto my bed.

"Anyplace I can smoke?" Jacob asked. "It was a long drive."

I was grateful for a reason to walk back outside. Halfway down the stairs, though, I grew anxious about Peggy up in the suite with Elena. What would they talk about? Which of my secrets would they let slip to one another?

I'd never smoked a cigarette before. Being completely "substance-free" was 80 percent of my identity in high school, with the other 20 percent filled in by the Catholic Church. I leaned on the cool metal banister behind the building, showed Jacob the designated smoking area. We were alone.

This young man across from me with the five o'clock shadow and military-buzz haircut was not quite a stranger. I recognized pieces of the boy I'd known—the high round cheeks, his rat-a-tat giggle, the steel in his gaze when he concentrated. But the hairline retreating up his forehead and the broadness of his shoulders were new. I only knew the most basic facts of his life. After he left Oklahoma, my brother had been shuffled between family members in South Jersey. He'd lived with Michael until his second year of high school, but then moved in with our grandmother

Hall when Michael and his new wife moved. That lasted until Jacob got caught shoplifting and Grandmother Hall kicked him out. When no one else wanted him, he was finally allowed to move in with Peggy for his last year of high school. He joined the National Guard, then the Army.

"Not a lot of smokers here, huh?" Jacob said.

"Everyone's obsessed with looking healthy," I replied.

My brother nodded, and leaned into his cigarette like I was leaning on the banister. It was a familiar thing to him, a piece of his world that he brought into this one. I felt shitty for wearing a pink skirt, for my flat-ironed hair, for the obvious way this place was me reaching away from him. I was still like him; we could share things.

"Gimme one," I said, my open palm closing the distance between us.

Jacob smiled. The dimples in his cheeks popped as he pursed his lips to light a cigarette for me. He knew I wouldn't do it properly. For a moment it was like we were in high school and he was my big brother teaching me to smoke. He'd rather I do these things with him than with strangers, he might have said. We could have been behind a school building, sandwiched between a brick wall and a dumpster, hiding our hands from the prying eyes of the campus rent-a-cops. I might have had my first sip of alcohol with him, too. Gone to my first party. He would have forbidden me from dating any of his friends. *They're all assholes*, he would have said.

If we were those people, that's how it would have been.

Through our jagged veil of smoke, we watched the families on the quad; with my brother beside me they suddenly seemed absurd. Their smiles unnaturally bright, their handbags too big, comically large, their affection for one another so demonstrative that it felt staged.

"These people are a friggin' riot," Jacob said. "We better get back up there and rescue your roommate." He stubbed his cigarette out on the sole of his shoe, and carefully discarded the butt in a garbage can.

Back in my room, Peggy and Elena lounged in two giant inflatable armchairs. "These were the last two in the back-to-school aisle," Peggy said when I opened the door. "I saw the kids in Jersey snapping 'em up, and I held these back for my Mary." She pushed herself up from the rubbery chair so eagerly that she nearly lost her balance. She hurried to show me the other gifts—microwave-safe dishes and mugs, a pair of black boots, a forest-green blanket that she'd crocheted for me, a Phillies cap.

"So you don't forget where you came from." Jacob giggled as he stuffed the hat on my head.

She shouldn't have bought so much, but I couldn't say that. Her smile wouldn't let me. The possibility of our old intimacy was too dazzling.

"She was gonna bring more, but she didn't know how big your room was."

"I didn't know what you had already," Peggy corrected.

From the depths of one of the purple chairs, Elena giggled. It bristled the hair on the back of my neck. In Oklahoma, having an audience was what enabled Mimi and Granddad and I to behave like a family, but in this case the presence of Elena was intrusive. Jacob, Peggy, and I had just gotten the old band back together and we weren't ready to perform for the public.

We lunched at an Italian restaurant with red-checkered table-cloths, far from campus. Peggy beamed at me from across the table and I was reminded of how I had owned her as a child, how her body was my body, her hands my hands, the ways I would boss her and she would do what I said. *Lemme play with your hair, make me potatoes with things mixed inside, don't leave until I fall asleep.* This had not changed, somehow. If I demanded the rest of her pasta she would give it to me, if I insisted we leave this minute we would go. If I rolled my eyes at every word she said, she would fall silent. There was nothing I could do that would raise a disagreeable word from her, nothing I could ask for that she would not find a way to give me.

What drove her was not entirely love, I understood then. There was something else, too. Something I learned in Catholic school, something I saw in Granddad, as well: it was guilt. I swore into my bowl of fettuccine that I would never ask Peggy for more than she could afford to give.

We returned to campus after dark. When we got back to the suite, Elena was sitting at her desk.

"I wouldn't be doing my duty as a big brother if I leave without teaching you somethin'," Jacob said. "You gotta know how to handle yourself, a' right?"

He demonstrated some martial arts moves that he'd learned in the Army.

He instructed me and Elena how to use the sharpest part of our radius bone to break free if someone grabbed us by the wrist, how to escape if someone approached from behind. "If some football player gets in your face and won't leave you alone, stick your finger under his nose like this." He pressed his index finger between my top lip and my nose, and immediately my head snapped back.

Elena and Peggy laughed from the side of the room. They

didn't know why Jacob was so serious about self-defense, why this was the thing he felt compelled to teach me in our day together. They didn't see that he was one scared kid trying help another scared kid not be afraid of the things that lurked in the dark.

A FEW days later I returned to my room after class to find a stack of messages on my desk. In my roommates' varied handwriting they all read, *Your dad called.* When I called the house on Forty-fourth Street, though, Granddad said he hadn't. We waded through ten minutes of small talk to reach a place where we could politely say goodbye. After we hung up, I checked my voice mail. There was a message from a Michael. Except he didn't introduce himself as Michael, he started the message with, "Hello, Mary, it's Daddy," his voice buoyant and sunshiny. I hadn't heard from him in years.

In the voice mail Michael said Peggy had told him how to reach me. He said he was sad that I hadn't thought to invite him up for Family Weekend, too. I didn't call him back because I didn't know what to say. Over the course of the week, my voice mail box filled up.

I finally checked it on Friday. The oldest messages were first. They were calm and even-toned. Had my roommates given me his messages? Michael wondered. He assumed they hadn't because I hadn't returned any of his calls. He reiterated his phone number. Call back. Call back, he said. On the next few messages, a twinge of doubt entered his voice. He wondered if I was avoiding him. I should know that he had wanted to call all those years ago, when I was in Oklahoma, but that Granddad and Mimi wouldn't let him. He was certain that any letters he sent were intercepted and never made it to me. I wondered if this was a crafted lie to cover the fact that he never sent any. Call back, he said.

In the messages after that, his voice grew tight and high-pitched. "People" had told him that I was upset that he didn't send birthday presents when I was a kid, but I should know that he was unemployed for many of those years. I had no idea what "people" he meant. Possibly Peggy? Or Jacob? Perhaps his own guilt suggested this to him. Call back, he said.

In the final voice mails he was strident, righteous. Maybe I didn't recall the Fifth Commandment, *Honor your father and mother*, he accused. He reminded me of the fact that the phone works both ways. Why hadn't I called him all those years I was gone? Why hadn't I sent him any presents? Had I thought of that? I should think about how selfish I am and repent.

What kept me hooked as each message bled into the next was the hope that I would hear regret in his voice. I wanted Michael to say he was sorry for losing me, for losing my sisters, for not being better, for giving up on us. The messiness of my life had to be someone's fault. Even if all the blame didn't land on Michael, there were still many things I could forgive him for. But was it possible to forgive someone when they never asked for it? Or does unrequested absolution become a self-inflicted wound? These questions snuck into my psyche that day, though I wasn't ready to ask them out loud. I wasn't ready to ask any questions that I didn't know the answer to. I didn't delete the messages from Michael; I didn't want him to have the space to leave more of them.

While I listened to his messages, Abigail, Sadie, and Elena were on the other side of the room mixing diet Coke with vanilla vodka and assessing one another's outfits in the full-length mirror, deliberating over boots and fleeces. Classes were done for the week, the snow had barely begun to fall. It was Friday night and no matter how old I felt, or how panicked I was at being berated by my estranged father, I could grab on to that. It was Friday night, I was eighteen years old, my roommates were going to a party, and I would join them. Because that is what eighteen-year-olds did. They put on fresh eyeliner, borrowed their girl-friend's sweater, and they went out.

It would be my first real college party, my first party where there was sure to be beer and vats of spiked punch. I had never been able to separate drinking from the sad, drunk adults of my childhood, the sweaty oblivion that played across their faces as they guzzled bottles malt liquor, alongside the fear of what would come out of me if I lost my self control. But something inside me craved that tonight. Something inside me knew that booze was just the thing to quiet the dull thudding in my gut.

Abigail looked at me through the mirror and said, "You really want to go?"

"Absolutely," I said, taking a long pull from the spiked diet Coke bottle. "I want to get hammered."

Like a Hole in My Head

After that, I partied like a college girl. Which is to say, probably a little too much.

I picked up a boyfriend at the beginning of my sophomore year. We met during a musical revue put on by the Student Musical Theatre Company. After a few beers at the cast party, I kissed him just to see if I was capable of it, and he wouldn't let me forget it. Joshua was achingly normal. He designed posters and played guitar. He was a charismatic, gentle boy who was prone to professions of love. Though he was willing to stick to saying, "I like you a great deal," when he saw me cringe repeatedly at the *l*-word. He showed up at my lunch table in the dining hall and in my pew at Sunday Mass. He wrote songs for me and slid mix CDs under my door. He became so ubiquitous that one day while walking on the quad I realized I was holding his hand, only I couldn't remember who had reached for whom.

I'd begun my sophomore year in the highly coveted position as a resident advisor. Even kids who weren't on work-study wanted to be RAs because you got to live in a giant single room with the shortest walk to class. I liked those perks, but what I enjoyed most was that my residents needed me, even if it was only because I was the person who signed out the vacuum cleaner.

I was on duty on a Tuesday night in early September when my life changed forever. It was my job that night to walk three laps through the freshman dorms and keep my door open until midnight in case any residents needed something. Most of my residents would be busy with practices and study groups until nine o'clock or later. The building would be quiet until then; I'd have plenty of time to finish a paper for my poetry class before I'd have to enforce quiet hours. But I made the mistake of checking my email before I settled into my desk and began my work.

The first unread message was from an account I didn't recognize. The subject line read, *Hello.* I saw the first sentence in the preview panel:

My name is Lisa. You don't know me, but you've known about me your entire life.

MY HEART beat fast. I was hot. I ripped my wool sweater from my body so quickly that it caught on my ears. I sat back in my desk chair. No. I needed to stand up, twitch, pace. The reflection in my bay window was foreign. It seemed as if I were watching myself and also gazing at a stranger. I lay on the floor, where I couldn't see any part of me.

I don't know how long I lay on my floor staring at the ceiling. Along with the walls, it had been repainted weeks before I moved into this room. The carpet, the furniture, everything had been cleaned or replaced, erasing any trace of the previous occupant. When I moved out of this room, there would be no hint of me, either.

I shook the leg of my desk until the cordless phone fell off its dock and into reaching distance. Then I dialed Becca in her dorm at Oklahoma State, but I got her voice mail. To reach Jacob I'd have to call Michael's house and I wasn't ready for that, and calling Peggy . . . I didn't want to do that until I knew what to say.

I'd thought I had more time. Lisa, the oldest of my long-lost little sisters, would not have been old enough to legally search for her birth family until March of my senior year of college, which was when she would turn eighteen. That's what I had planned for. My sisters were supposed to find me when I was teaching English in Japan, interning at a congressional office, or starting law school. I didn't have the particulars planned yet. All I knew was that I would be well adjusted when my sisters found me. But now she was here, and I was still me: nineteen years old and confused.

One by one my residents repopulated the building. Their voices caught in the corners of the hallway and bounced into my room. Doors slapped open and closed, open and closed. I started to breathe in rhythm with them. Open and closed, open and closed, in and out, in and out.

I stood up and stared deep into my computer screen, read the rest of the message. Lisa's parents had agreed to help her search for us. It wasn't a long process because they knew Michael's full name and he hadn't moved far. She called him on the phone, though they hadn't yet met. He gave her my email address. She couldn't believe I was so close.

WITHOUT SOMEONE else to watch react to this news, I wasn't sure how I felt. In fact, I was certain that I didn't feel anything. My nerve endings seized, in the midst of a psychological reboot.

Every system in my body needed to be updated with this new information.

I've been found, I've been found.

Becca called me the following morning. She'd gotten an email, too. I called Peggy. Jacob was at her place and we all arranged to meet Lisa at Peggy's apartment over Thanksgiving weekend. It would be the first time the four of us were together since the day I'd left New Jersey twelve years before.

Peggy lived in a two-bedroom apartment with her longtime boyfriend, Tom. Their place was above the pizza shop that Tom ran with his brother. The apartment was always filled with the warm smell of yeasted dough emanating from the shop below. I'd stayed with them the year before over Thanksgiving, too. In the mornings, Tom took me down to the shop and showed me how to make pizza dough in the giant mixer at the back kitchen, how to portion it, proof it, and place individual dough balls in flat racks with the date and my initials on them. "That way, if there's anything wrong with 'em, we'll know whose ass to kick," he'd said in his dusky monotone. He wasn't kidding.

It was simple, honest work, and Tom took pride in it. He could not have been more different from Michael. Where Michael was gregarious, creative, and scheming, Tom was quiet, steady, and generous. Until I saw Peggy with Tom, I hadn't realized how depressed she must have been when I was a kid. I no longer saw her sleep late into the day or sit at the kitchen table with her head in her hands. Now she was up in the mornings making pancakes for breakfast. Unlike our apartments in Marigold Court and Camden, here Peggy hung things on the walls. She decorated with pinecones and bottles of herb-infused olive oil, chattering pleasantly about where she had found this trinket or who had given her that jar of peppers. Except for the fact that I didn't know anyone she mentioned, it felt familiar, homey.

I couldn't help thinking that this was what we could have been like. If Peggy had met and married Tom instead of Michael, I could have stayed with her. I could have grown up to be like one of Tom's sisters, mouthy but charming, telling people to sit down while I fixed them a plate.

On the day of the reunion, Jacob, Becca, and I sipped coffee around Peggy's kitchen table while she fussed with pot holders on the countertop. "I can't sit still," she said, pouring herself a glass of water.

"Ma, you already have two glasses of water," Jacob said, and pointed to one glass on the table and one on the countertop. "You gotta sit down before you have a heart attack."

Peggy gulped from the glass in her hand and placed it in the sink. She shook her head and smiled. "I'm fine," she said. But her voice wavered and she kept rubbing her hands.

I was glad for the solidity of the oak table. Without it to cling to, I was certain that I would float away like a helium balloon, out the window and through the atmosphere, higher and higher, until the too-thin air crushed me.

Jacob and Becca were subdued by matching hangovers. When I had taken a dose of cold medicine and gone to bed early the night before, my brother and sister went to a party at one of Jacob's friends' house, where Becca had snorted some cocaine. Just a bump, she said. But when she was still wide awake at four in the morning, she started downing whiskey to counteract its effect and Jacob joined her. They sat pale and glassy-eyed at opposite ends of the table. In twenty-four hours Becca would be headed back to Oklahoma State University and Jacob was scheduled to ship out to a U.S. base in Germany after Christmas. It seemed like a waste of time to be pissed about the previous night's shenanigans; I focused instead on being grateful that they'd left time to shower.

I felt my new sister's presence before I saw her. There was a knock on the door and suddenly my head filled with a ringing tone so loud I could feel it in my fillings. I didn't think I was the only person who felt it, but before I could check with Becca and Jacob, Peggy had opened the door and Lisa was standing in the kitchen with us.

Her strawberry blond hair hung past her shoulders. She was big-eyed, with impeccable highlights, expertly applied eye makeup, and a set of acrylic nails that clicked against each other in a rhythm that I recalled from the mothers of Marigold Court in my childhood. In her snug jeans, boots, and V-neck sweater, Lisa looked more mature than me. Her eyes were the same shade of blue-green as Becca's, but the rest of her face was a carbon copy of mine. The slope of her nose and the round doll-like shape of her eyes were mine. Granddad would never have let me out of the house in that sweater, though. Not when I was Lisa's age, and not now.

We moved into the living room and I caught a glimpse of us—Jacob, Becca, Lisa, and me—side by side in the mirror above the sofa. In that moment we appeared oldest to youngest, our hair and eyes getting progressively lighter as though the dye wore off with subsequent washings. I felt it in my stomach, in the mess of viscera in my gut: the sudden knowledge of another being who was like me, part of me.

I had focused so long on my goal of her finding me that I never considered how I would react to her presence. I hadn't thought about what it would feel like to look into Lisa's face, hadn't counted on her face looking back at me so . . . expectantly? Hopefully? Nervously? I had imagined that the act of being found would be the finish line, but now I could see that we were just at the beginning. Of a marathon.

On the other side of the room, Lisa's parents hugged the wall. They'd opened a door and they didn't know where it would lead. Could there be two mothers in the same room, or did they cancel one another out? We were all a little skittish, unsure of what roles to play, until Lisa's parents left.

After they left, we relaxed almost instantly. I was, for the first time, part of a club that I belonged to organically. I wanted to know everything about Lisa and she wanted to know everything about us. Peggy brought out photo albums. She pointed out cracked black-and-white pictures, saying, "This is your great-great-grandmother Durkin. She came over from County Sligo in Ireland during the famine," and "Here's your grandmother Taggart on Michael's side, her people were from Cork." Lisa clapped her thin hands together. "I always thought I was Irish! But I never knew for sure!"

When we got to the baby pictures of Becca, Lisa covered her mouth with her hands. "These look like pictures of me," she whispered. "It's like, it's like . . ." she sputtered and couldn't finish. She laughed as she wiped tears from her eyes. "It's so weird! It's awesome, but it's weird." I hummed my agreement.

I wanted more—the interior things, the thoughts and personality traits that wouldn't show up in photographs. I needed to know if Lisa laughed at the things I did, and if, like I did, she sometimes got so filled with rage she thought she could die. Did she have that dream that Becca, Jacob, and I all had, where her teeth fell out? If she did, was that just us? Or did everybody have that dream? Did her eyes water when she saw babies, was she good at tests? Was this us or everyone? I had no idea what characteristics belonged just to me, or to me and my family, or to everyone in the world.

I kept remembering the day, all those years ago, when Becca came to New Jersey. How she was sullen and sad when I was so happy. How that day was like so many of our days together since, with my sister and me committed to opposite emotions. But today we were all excited. Lisa did not point out the ways we didn't know her, and she did not turn away from us. She was game.

After the photo albums were finished, Jacob stretched up from the sofa.

"We should get going if she wants to meet Dad," he said.

I knew this was coming and had decided to be fine about it. I wouldn't say anything that might mar Lisa's first experience with our biological father. She had the right to make up her own mind about Michael. I wouldn't steal his chance to make a good first impression on his new daughter. Maybe he would be different with her.

Jacob drove us, in a minivan that he'd borrowed from Michael. Becca, Lisa, and I piled into the backseat. Peggy begged off, said she wanted to be home when Tom finished work for the night. But I suspected that she'd had enough reunion for one day. The thought of standing in the same house with her ex-husband and their ex-children would have been too much to bear.

In the middle of the White Horse Pike, Jacob turned on the radio and a song we all knew started playing. Becca, Lisa, and I instinctively sang the harmony parts. "Ohmygod," Lisa shrieked. "With my friends I'm always the one that sings harmony! You do that, too?" I was smiling so big that my jaw hurt.

In the minivan, we were a world unto ourselves. Wind shot through the van doors and it seemed that it had to reach into our pockets because we had too much energy that needed to be cooled somehow to keep us from spontaneously combusting. We were rosy from cold, rosy from warmth, like pomegranates, like summer peaches, like something I could sink my teeth into. The car windows fogged over. We were the stars and the clouds and the icy roads and the thud of bass and the *chikka-chikka-chikka* of the tire treads on the pavement. Nothing else that had happened before existed and nothing that would happen in the future mattered.

Until we reached Michael's house. I didn't want to get out of the car; I knew the spell would be broken once we did. But it was inevitable. We walked to the front door and Jacob knocked. Nobody answered, so he opened the door and stuck his head in.

"Pop?" he yelled through the house.

My sisters and I stepped over the threshold. We were in the living room, I guessed. The only furniture was a sagging sofa shoved against the wall and a few guitars in the left corner. I noticed a photo on the wall of Rebecca and me at our first Communion. Peggy must have given this to him; there was no way Mimi and Granddad would have sent Michael anything. It must have been hung for our benefit, or moved from another room, because dust settled on the wall in a way that suggested something larger and oval-shaped usually hung in this spot. It was exactly the sort of fumbled gesture I expected from Michael. I wanted to like it, wanted to let it land on me the way he intended, but I couldn't help scanning the room for whatever thing usually hung there.

Michael materialized from a doorway at the back corner of the room.

"Hey, sport!" he hummed, a fresh beer in his hand.

I recognized him from his movements: the sure-footed tromp, his wide-footed stance, the smirk through his beard. But his look had changed entirely; I wouldn't have known him if we sat beside each other on a bus. Michael's hair and beard were all silver. He had grown a potbelly. But it was his eyes that had changed the most. They didn't appear to focus on anything, at least not anything I could see. Had he always looked like he was peering into another world? Was I too young to notice this when I was a child, or was this new?

He came forward to hug me. I hugged him back so I wouldn't be weird, but all I could think was that I shouldn't have come here. I still had a handful of sepia-toned memories of Michael. Nights when he sang "Somewhere Over the Rainbow" until I fell asleep, the way he played "Monster Mash" for me whenever I accompanied him to deejay gigs, regardless of the season or the occasion. I remembered riding on his shoulders with my fingers twined into his scratchy beard. Seeing him now in this ramshackle house with his funny eyes and the wind blowing through a million cracks, I was sad. He was a stranger. I preferred to hold on to the handful of nice memories about him than to get to know this new, strange man.

A broad man with dirty blond hair followed Michael into the living room. "I go to church with your pop," was the only introduction he gave. He shuffled over to a corner of the room and sucked on a beer. He was here to watch, like we were a circus sideshow.

I sat on the sofa and Jacob joined me. Michael held Lisa out at arm's length, took in her features. "I remember the day you were born," he marveled. His eyes sparkled at her like they did when he used to talk about Jesus. His charisma pulled her toward him like a bug to a zapper. "Let me play you something," he said, grabbing one of the guitars in the corner. Michael sat cross-legged on the floor, the guitar in his lap. He waggled his feet so the steel toes of his boots hitting the wood floor provided percussion. It was a song he had written, about Jesus and being moved by the spirit, being given the gift of salvation. He closed his eyes, and when he reached for a high note his top lip jumped up to reveal his teeth. When the song was finished, his blond friend applauded from the corner.

"That's where we get it from!" Lisa said earnestly. "That was so cool."

"You think *that's* cool?" the blond guy said, like we were all suddenly buddies. "You wanna see cool, for real? Check out this hole in my head."

"What?" I said, in as nonpanicky a voice as I could manage.

"Got hit in the head with a hammer a few years back. Check it out."

"We have to get Lisa back to her parents . . ." I demurred.

"I'll touch it," Becca said.

I could have strangled her.

"A' right! You wanna get your finger riiiight there," the man coached as he offered the back of his head to Becca. He flipped his greasy locks to one side and revealed a large divot in his skull. "It's deeper than it looks. Get in there."

"Woah. That is deep," Becca said. Her eyes widened with shock.

After we left Michael and his friend, we picked Peggy up

at her apartment. We had to take Lisa back to her parents. We would meet them at the halfway point between Pine Beach and Haddonfield.

I sat in the backseat, with Lisa between Becca and me. When it was no longer simply our sibling group, the euphoria of being a world, alone, was lost. Doubt crept into my mind. Would this be the last we saw of Lisa, or would she keep in touch? Were we a surreal dream that she would rather forget?

Then the neon sign of our destination grew larger in the window frame of the windshield.

We were at Olga's Diner. The same place where, in 1985, we first met Lisa's parents. I hung back with Peggy as we walked in. It felt like we were going back in time. Lisa's parents were already there, sitting on the same side of a large booth. Lisa slid beside her parents, leaving the other side for us.

Sixteen years later, there was no disappointing husband, there were no children wandering under tables. The green vinyl booths were dumb witnesses to the closing of a genetic wormhole. Echoes of that other day panged across Peggy's face. Fragments of millions of thoughts were begun and discarded. She said only, "It was this booth. You sat over there." We sipped our coffee cups dry.

It had been a long day and Lisa had to get home. I shook hands with her parents. It felt strangely businesslike. But a hug would have been too familiar, wrong in a different way. Jacob, Becca, and I hugged Lisa. As I pulled away from my sister, her face was red and blotched. This was her first big goodbye. She was carving a spot inside herself now, I knew. A spot that, from this moment forward, would always feel half empty. We walked toward two separate vehicles headed in opposite directions.

Lisa sobbed in the parking lot. Like a character in a soap opera, she wallowed in it. I marveled at her lack of self-consciousness. Diner patrons watched her through the windows, wondering who had broken this pretty girl's heart. For that moment, we were merely props in Lisa's world. I felt myself slip out of our shared bubble and into my own, smaller one; out of focus and then back in again.

In the backseat of our car Becca cried and I put my head on her shoulder. Jacob's face was red in the rearview mirror but he didn't have any tears. Over the years since I'd lost my brother I had lost the ability to cry in front of other people, but every bone in my body pulsed with a dull ache like a giant fist had flattened me.

If everything went according to plan, this would happen three more times.

This was the best-case scenario. An instant connection, a day-long binge on genealogy, followed by a separation that tears a hole so deep in your psychic fabric that someday you'll encourage your friends' long-lost kids stick their fingers in it.

I returned to my single dorm room early Saturday morning. The building echoed with emptiness; most students wouldn't arrive back on campus until late the next day. They'd savor every moment they could with their families.

I was glad for the solitude so I could brace myself for my daily life, but then I sat down at my desk and saw a fresh email from Michael. He said he didn't think I cared to hear from him, so he'd keep the message short. In a page and half of ten-point type he told me that the reason he hadn't kept in touch throughout my childhood was because I had never done anything to make him feel that I cared about him. "People" had told him that I was "bitter" because he had never sent presents for holidays and birthdays. I couldn't imagine what people he meant, since only

Peggy and Jacob knew us both, and I couldn't picture these words coming from either one of them.

But if I wanted to hate him for the lack of gifts, that was my choice. It seemed a little "twisted around" in his opinion, though. I had never sent him any presents, either. He doubted that I even knew his birthday. He said he knew that I was planning to visit Peggy over Christmas break and if I was worried that he was mad about it, I should know that he definitely was not. This letter was simply to provide closure in his life, he said. He said he would always pray for me, but that as far as my being his daughter? Well, "that was destroyed long ago." Then he signed it "regards, Dad."

The message left me utterly cold. I wasn't angry, I wasn't sad in the way he clearly wanted me to be. It was a retread of his voicemail vitriol from the year before. He was wrong about some timelines and wrong about my Christmas plans, but he was right about a few things. I didn't know his birthday. I didn't even know his middle name. And as for me being his daughter . . . I couldn't have said it better myself; that was destroyed long ago. It was a repeat of all his accusations from the year before. More than anything I was simply bored with retreading the same territory. He couldn't stop himself from signing the missive with the surreal "Dad." Out of habit, I guessed. I didn't know how to address him—Michael? Dad?—so I skipped a title of any kind and wrote what I felt was true.

I do not bear you any ill will, anger, or bitterness. Our paths in life split a very long time ago, and today, I simply do not know you, nor do you know me. I think if we are honest, we would agree on that. It has nothing to do with presents, birthdays, or phone calls. I do not recall your birthday because I

*never remember celebrating it with you. You found a place in
a family that needed you, and so did I. And now we both have
very full lives and seem to be taking care of ourselves just fine.*

*I don't wish to keep revisiting this issue every few years, and
think it would be best if you let it go, as I have.*

*Thank you for the good wishes; I wish nothing but good
things for you and your family as well.*

Mary

I read it several times before I sent it and was stunned by the
seeming maturity of the language. It came more from exhaustion
than from anything else. The part about my finding a place in a
family that needed me overstated my situation with Mimi and
Granddad, I felt, but in my final message to my ex-father I felt a
need to convince him that I was at least as well loved as he was.

When I woke up in my dorm room the next morning, my
throat was coiled tight. I coughed streaks of blood into my hand
before breakfast. I was at the intake desk of Student Health Services before I realized that my throat was too rigid to talk. Words
came out as an insubstantial whistle of air.

The doctor diagnosed my ailment as "laryngitis caused by
gastro-esophageal reflux." He gave me pills and told me to avoid
coffee and spicy food. I walked back up the hill to my dorm room,
bottles of ibuprofen and antacids jostling in my pockets. Joshua
arrived in my room that evening armed with both soup and ice
cream, saying he'd eat whichever one I didn't want.

In that moment, silence was my friend once again. When
Joshua asked what I did over Thanksgiving break, I didn't have
to say, *My ex-father broke up with me*, or *I was in a world of icy roads
and fogged windows*. Through finals week I remained mute. My

doctor scoped my throat; my vocal cords were too swollen and inflamed to operate properly. He wrote me a note so my professors wouldn't think I was faking and prescribed a stricter diet of bread, bananas, rice, toast—things even babies can eat.

In the final weeks of the fall semester, I found myself mentally blanking out in the middle of conversations. Friends joked that I was becoming scatterbrained. Sad movies—sometimes even sad commercials—could send me into an earnest depression for the rest of the day, like I was a delicate character from a Louisa May Alcott novel. All of these qualities led Joshua and my friends to grander demonstrations of affection. They made a point to invite me on shopping trips to Syracuse, to parties and art history lectures. Fellow resident advisors dropped by my room on their nightly rounds. Everyone thought I was depressed because I couldn't sing, or that I was experiencing a particularly violent bout of homesickness. Both were somewhat true, I supposed.

Good Daughter

I graduated from college with a degree in English and a minor in political science, broke up with Joshua, and I headed back to the house on Forty-fourth Street to plan my next move. By that point I was leading what felt like a triple life. I was Mary the successful student, Mary the oldest sister in a growing brood of the lost and found, and—as some of the parishioners at Holy Redeemer Catholic Church referred to me when I visited on holidays—I was Mary, Charles and Mimi King's "good daughter."

The "good daughter" always made me cringe a little, for what it insinuated about Becca. It couldn't be a compliment to me without being an insult to her. But I mostly hated the moniker because it came with so much responsibility and, quite frankly, I wasn't sure it was true. I'd left them behind when I went off to college. Becca was the one who stayed in state. She was the daughter they saw more than once a year.

As I negotiated my suitcase through the screen door and onto the porch, I adjusted my purse strap more firmly on my shoulder. I had a letter in there, a job offer, from a company that wanted me to teach English for them in Japan. All I had to do was sign the thing and mail it back. Four years ago I had wished for precisely this prize—a good-paying job that made me sound interesting. I hadn't told anyone about it yet. I just had to get through this summer with a little money in my pocket. Then I'd be halfway around the world saying, *Konnichiwa*, and eating real sushi for the first time.

When I opened the front door I expected to smell Mimi's favorite potpourri of furniture polish and glass cleaner, but what I got was a nose full of dust. The curtains that should have been taken down and cleaned every thirty days were covered in a thin layer of grit. I could write my name in the film that had settled on top of the china presses. The deep shag carpet had lost its springy volume. Mimi's dolls, her treasured creations high atop the cabinets, were shrouded in cobwebs.

The floorboards sighed and creaked as I walked in. I heard voices coming from the kitchen.

"No, I can *do* it."

"Let me help."

I parked my suitcase at the base of the stairs and followed the trail of tubing from Mimi's oxygen tank to the back of the house. When I got to the kitchen I saw Mimi on the floor in a pair of pink pajamas, Granddad hovering over her like a nervous sheepdog. I tumbled in as Mimi gripped a chair and pulled herself up. She smiled at me and said, "Well, look what the cat drug in!"

I barely recognized her. She had gained twenty pounds, all in her cheeks and her stomach. But her limbs were still thin as toothpicks. "It's the steroids they've got her on," Granddad said. "They put meat on her bones and make her stubborn."

Mimi had always been stubborn; she didn't need steroids for that. Looking at her now, I realized that the times I had come home to visit she must have been putting on a show, acting strong and pretending to be fine. But she was weak, thin, and frail. Her voice had a crackling quality to it now, as if under her breath I could hear her lungs crunching like paper bags. She started coughing and didn't stop for ten minutes.

"Sounds like you need your next breathing treatment," Granddad said.

Mimi waved him off. "Oh, Charles, I'm fine."

I clutched my purse tight under my arm and heard the letter crinkle. *Now's not the time*, I thought. I'd wait to tell them that I didn't plan to stay long. After Mimi lay down for a nap, I started to carry my suitcase up to my old bedroom and Granddad stopped me.

"It's Mimi's sewing room now," he said shyly.

"But she can't get up there, can she?" I asked in a whisper from the first set of stairs.

"No," he said, "but it's important that she thinks she will someday." He looked wrung out. I wanted things to work easily and would go where I was pointed. There was no sense in being stung about the fact that my sanctuary had been overtaken; it was their house and I was the one who left.

"I'm fine with Becca's room," I said and dragged my things into the downstairs bedroom. There had been changes here, too. Gone was the queen-sized bed that Becca and I had slept in fifteen years ago. In its place were two twin beds with matching beige sheets and white blankets. This was a guest bedroom now, a place for visitors. But from the look of the place, with the same coating of dust that matched the rest of the house, no visitors had been by in quite some time. I left most of my things in boxes that I tucked under the beds. They could stay there for the next two years while I was across the world becoming someone more interesting, I figured. It wasn't as if Mimi and Granddad were going anywhere.

I registered with a temp agency that afternoon. I needed to get a job quickly so I could fund my move. At the house I cooked dinner, did laundry, and attempted to clean the place up to Mimi's standards. I learned how to prepare her twice-daily breathing treatments, helped her with her shoes, and clipped her toenails. I had grown familiar with her body by now, I knew the places where she needed her shoulder rubbed when she woke up in the morning, the weird way the toenails on her second toes curved when they were allowed to grow too long. I didn't wonder then—as I would many years later—whether I did these things out of affection or guilt. At the time I was convinced that I did them because they needed to be done. And that was enough.

Jolene still came every Saturday to curl Mimi's hair. She brought homemade fudge and little pink journals with notes in the front, cheerfully suggesting that Mimi record some of the stories she knew about her family. Mimi nodded when she leafed through the blank pages, but the books remained empty beside her recliner in Granddad's den. I don't know if she balked because she didn't like that the suggestion implied that she was dying, or if she simply lacked the energy to write.

I'd been home for a week when I accompanied Mimi and Granddad to one of Mimi's doctor visits. There was an escalator from the lobby of the building to the second floor. I strode confidently aboard with Mimi's portable oxygen tank on my left shoulder, her left arm braced against my right arm. I turned back to ask Granddad the suite number and saw that he was two steps behind me, with his shoulder turned away as if to camouflage the look of abject terror on his face as he attempted to place his feet squarely on the moving steps. When had he gotten so old?

In the appointment, Mimi's pulmonologist suggested that intravenous drugs would more effectively halt the scar tissue building up in her lungs. Mimi pursed her lips. *No hospitals*. Hospitals were where people went to die, and she was not dying. She was just sick. "It is possible to administer the drugs at home, if your family is up for it," the doctor said, indicating Granddad and me. We nodded. Of course we were. Mimi hadn't hesitated to do the million little things she'd done for me, and how hard could it be? The doctor inserted a port in Mimi's left arm and sent us home with the assurance that he would complete the necessary arrangements.

The next day a gray apparatus the size of a cinder block arrived at the house along with bags of fluid and syringes with snub-nosed ends that fit snugly into the accompanying tubes. I devoured the diagrams with their yellow triangles screaming *CAUTION!*, determined not to make a mistake. After dinner we set Mimi up on one of the beds in my room, snapped the tubing into her arm port, and followed the diagrams. Granddad looked over my shoulder while I first flushed the line with one syringe of heparin (*CAUTION: Watch for air bubbles*), followed that with the tube of warfarin, (*CAUTION: double check labels! DO NOT double HEPARIN!*), then plopped the pouch of steroids into the gray plastic machine, rolled it around the squeegee (*CAUTION: Ensure the bag is placed snugly below the roller!*), snapped it closed, and waited for it to hum (*CAUTION: If the machine does not hum, no fluid is being dispensed!*).

Once the humming began, I lay on the other twin bed and watched the squeegee roll over the bag of fluid. The full dose was supposed to take an hour. But it didn't look like the fluid was going up the tube. It was just getting squeezed, like a giant blister about to pop under the pressure. I stopped the apparatus, popped it open. Rewrapped, resnapped, waited for the hum. It wasn't working. It took two more attempts and several phone calls to the Ask-a-Nurse help line to get the full dose administered that night. It was four o'clock in the morning by the time it finished, and a blood-colored bruise had developed on Mimi's arm where the IV was inserted.

Looking at it made my eyes burn. I wasn't sure if it was because I was failing, or because nothing I did could make this better. I was relieved when the doctor scheduled a real nurse to come every two days and deal with the IV.

I missed Becca. The house on Forty-fourth Street reverberated with echoes of her. The spindly tools that she had once used to pry popcorn hulls out of her braces were still in the medicine cabinet. Her VHS copies of *Titanic* and *Empire Records* sat on the bottom shelf of the bookcase in the hall. I could only use half the hanging rods in my closet because her winter coats and prom dresses still hung there. They smelled like the patchouli oil that she had bought in the arts district. I always hated that swampy aroma. I still hated it, but because it was my sister's scent I stuck my face in the ghostly silks and satins and breathed in until I gagged. Becca and I had become friends again the night we'd met Lisa. We'd shared a room that night and whispered back and forth about how surreal it was. I hadn't expected to feel so drawn to our new sister, and neither had she.

After Becca dropped out of Oklahoma State a year and a half before, she'd moved from one small rural town to another, snaking her way down to the far southwest corner of the state. I'd been home for three weeks before I made the drive down to Lawton to see her in her new place. She'd started playing with a band, a punk-rock metal group of four girls, and she invited me to a Friday night show. My plan was to see her and then nudge her to come back to Oklahoma City with me.

All I knew about Becca's new town was that it was home to a small Army base, Fort Sill, and more meth labs per capita than any other place in the state. There was also a tiny college where we were meant to think that Becca was taking classes so she could transfer back to Oklahoma State. I'd never been this far southwest in Oklahoma. I'd never intended to live in this state long enough to be considered "from" it, and figured the less I steeped myself in its history and culture, the better. There was a stark honesty in the bleak flatness of the place. What you saw was what you got. And, usually, what you got was a spot devoid of any place to hide.

For two hours down the desolate highway, I ran through my plan for the night. I'd hit the concert, then we'd pile onto Becca's sofa and watch the PBS late-night movie over a bag of Becca's favorite buttered popcorn that I had packed for the occasion. I'd stay in Becca's apartment for the night, then talk her into coming back to OKC with me for a visit. Once I had her in Mimi and Granddad's house, I'd show her the ropes for being around Mimi. How to administer medicines and help her with her exercises. Once she wasn't so freaked out by Mimi's illness, Becca could, I thought, be a better nurse than I was. More comfortable.

I pulled into the parking lot of the coffee shop hosting the concert. It was a quaint lavender building. As I walked toward the entrance I saw a pack of sunburned shirtless guys sitting in the bed of a beat-down Dodge pickup. They passed around a bottle of Mad Dog. They were in their twenties, but only had one full set of teeth between the four of them. They could tell from my white capri pants that I wasn't from around here.

"Miss . . ." One shirtless guy tipped his head in a small salute as I passed. These guys might be blind drunk, but they could still act like gentlemen. "Ho-leee hell!" he said, taking a closer look at me. "You're Becca's sister, ain't you? You want some Mad Dog?"

I shook my head. "I'll get a coffee inside," I said. "But thank you."

When I walked in I couldn't find my sister anywhere. I saw her bandmates, though, setting up equipment and tuning their instruments. Becca always made friends with everybody, especially the sort of individuals most people wouldn't hurry to sit next to on the subway—pen-ink tattoos at the base of their necks, piercings on every available facial feature, grimy gums, and serpentine skin. The group gathering in the coffee shop was hitting all the usual marks.

At eight-thirty Becca ran in the front door in a pair of hip-hugging black pants covered all over in red plaid zippers, and a black spaghetti-strap tank top that showed a sliver of her belly all the way around her waistband. There wasn't a stage at the coffee shop, and there was only one microphone. With the drum kit set up in the corner and the amps for the two guitars, the thirty people gathered in the shop came close enough to touch the band. They started to play. The venue was far too small for their full drum set; the percussion flattened the rest of the instruments and vocals into an unintelligible mess. I couldn't hear my sister's lead guitar at all, but I could see that she had lost twenty pounds since the last time I'd seen her and the teeth Granddad had spent so much money to straighten had spread back into disarray.

After the last song, the lead singer, a raven-haired sprite in a red dress, screeched, "Party at Zack and Eddie's! Let's go!" That got the loudest cheer of the night.

After the band carried amps and thick coils of cord to the parking lot, I found myself driving in a caravan headed to an apartment complex across town.

"Who are Zack and Eddie?" I asked Becca as I drove. I hoped they weren't the Mad Dog guys.

"They're cool, they're in the Army; like Jay," she said. Her eyes were glassy in the passing streetlights. I could see deep pits in the skin along her cheekbones.

"I thought we'd watch the late-night movie. It's supposed to be *Casablanca* tonight," I said. *Casablanca* had been our favorite vintage film. When we were in high school we'd take turns swanning around the living room saying, *Play it again, Sam*, while the other sister practiced piano.

"I forgot you were such a dork," Becca snorted in the passenger seat.

"I came to see you," I said as the paved road gave way to gravel and the proper buildings of the town disappeared behind us. "You, not a bunch of strangers . . ."

"It's really important to me that you meet my friends," Becca said. "They're like my family." As if we didn't have enough family for numerous lifetimes. I parked behind a half-lit brick-crete building on the edge of town. In the center of the complex was a fenced-in pool, drained even in the summer heat.

"It's awesome to skate in," Becca marveled. "Better than if it even had water in it."

She had a faraway look in her eyes, as if she were tracking a distant star. It was an expression I recognized from Michael's face.

We walked through the weed-studded sidewalk to a dim, humid apartment. The smell was a combination of stale beer, vomit that was never fully cleaned out of the carpet, the musk of collective body odor, and the acid tang of waste seeping through old pipes. "You made it!" a scrawny shirtless boy—Zack or Eddie?—crowed when we walked in the door. He had more tattoos on his torso than he had furniture in his home. Every countertop was covered in foot-high layers of plastic cups and pizza boxes. He was hosting ecosystems in here.

Thirty or forty people were already crammed into the tiny space and everyone was covered in sweat. Half the girls wandered through the room in stained bras; the guys were all bare-chested. The doors and windows were all open. I was, it seemed, the only one here who was not fucked up. My craving for a drink was eclipsed by my desire to get the hell out of here.

I stepped back into the courtyard to breathe in some less rank oxygen. The Mad Dog guys from the coffee shop were running laps around the parking lot, barefoot. Dust and dirt caked past their ankles. Hypodermic needles glinted below the dead bushes underneath the front windows of Zack and Eddie's apartment.

Finally, we left.

Becca's apartment at least had a couch and a TV. But the place was covered in layers of dirty clothes that soaked the patchouli scent off her body and spread it around her apartment. My sister only did laundry once a month. She stretched that time by purchasing economy-sized packs of cotton underwear from Wal-Mart. Her cupboards held nothing but paper plates, empty mason jars, and an unopened bag of brown rice flour. In the pantry were more jars and a half-full bag of potting soil. The fridge held two beers and the dregs of a bottle of Mountain Dew.

In the freezer I found a cardboard box. It had been opened in a frenzy; the side of the box was scooped round in the shape of fingers. I pulled it out to inspect it more closely. I expected neat envelopes of frozen burritos or breakfast pastries, but I saw syringes. Twenty-four plastic syringes full of some clear liquid that had gone syrupy from the cold. The tags affixed to each one read PSILOCYBE CUBENSIS SPORES. Instead of food, my sister had syringes of . . . fungus?

She was sad, I thought, or angry and scared; it was hard to tell. Every time I saw her those days she was smoking a cigarette or a joint or drunk or on acid or coke or mushrooms or speed. I should have understood: she was trying to erase herself, to disappear. That was a desire I knew. But because my own strategies for self-erasure were socially acceptable things—books, music, church—I failed to see that our motivations were identical. I smacked the wall between the kitchen and her bedroom. "Hey!" I said, "Why do you have spores in your freezer?"

Becca came into the kitchen, saw the box on the countertop.

"It's for a biology class I'm taking."

"Twenty-four syringes of the same fungus?"

"We're looking at them under microscopes and stuff," she said.

I stalked through her tiny apartment; she followed me. I scanned the floors and flat surfaces for any sort of student paraphernalia.

"Where are your books?" I accused.

A college biology textbook would weigh eight pounds. It would be bigger than a Bible. There would be notebooks, flash cards, an array of highlighters and click-top pens.

"They're . . . in the trunk of my car."

"You must be studying a lot," I scoffed.

"I study enough." She blew hair off her sticky forehead.

It was late. I was tired from the drive and frazzled by the concert; I didn't want to fight with her. "I smell like other people's sweat," I said. "I'm taking a shower."

By the time I was clean, Becca was asleep, or pretending to be. I nudged her leg with my foot. I hoped she would wake up and we could talk like we had in Peggy's guest room the night after we met Lisa. Like we used to do when we were kids. But I got nothing.

In the morning my sister said, "Mind if I don't go with you today?"

Her face was ashen and her voice flat. Whatever had lifted her mood and body temperature last night had worn off. "I'm not really feeling like a long drive, you know?" I told her I didn't mind.

"If we weren't sisters, you think we'd even be friends?" she asked.

"I don't know," I said. "Does it matter? We *are* sisters."

Becca shrugged and promised she would visit Mimi soon.

On my way back, I turned over the events of the night. Becca wasn't too afraid to see Mimi; she was too fucked up. On methamphetamine, I assumed. I had to assume, because meth was too lowbrow to be included in my drug training as an RA; the affluent kids at my college were more likely to snort Adderall or smoke weed than get hooked on a drug that hillbillies cooked in their trailers. I assumed because by not outright asking I could still pretend I didn't know.

Mimi and Granddad deserved a good daughter. They'd given up their retirement to buy Becca and me school shoes and plane tickets. When I studied abroad for a semester in London, Granddad put a thousand dollars into my bank account just because, just so I would have it. They deserved someone to be good to them. No one asked me to stay; the only thing forcing me was my own guilty conscience. Accepting help obligated a person. I couldn't be half a world away when Mimi was dying, I knew. I made myself say it out loud, like a doctor in a waiting room. *Mary, your mother is dying.* Those were the roles we were cast in. Whatever we called one another, Mimi had taken me in, cared for me, and that meant that I owed her.

The first thing I did when I got in the house was find my letter for that job in Japan. Standing in the kitchen, I took one last look at it, then balled it up and threw it in the garbage.

Two days later Peggy called. She had called before I left for Lawton, too. We'd do this dance every month or two where she called every few days until she caught me. I wasn't avoiding her, but I did always hesitate to call back. Most of what I had to talk about would be Mimi's condition, and Becca's annoying absence. It was impossible to mention those names to Peggy without opening wounds. Peggy might bristle that Mimi and Granddad had spoiled Rebecca. That they thought my sister's acting out was a result of Peggy's rebellious genes expressing themselves, *But look at who raised us both*, Peggy would say. I could hear the defensive shrug in her voice.

I was gearing up for just such a conversation when Peggy said, "I just got off the phone with Rebecca."

I rested my forehead on my hands.

"Did she say I was rude to her friends?" I bristled, ready to defend myself. "Did she tell you what her friends were *like?*"

"Not Becca," Peggy said. "*Re*-bekah. Rebekah Two. Little Rebekah."

The adrenaline that pumped through my veins was redirected. The repeat, the echo, the record skipping. Rebekah.

Peggy planned to meet her this weekend in New Jersey. Jacob was home on leave from the Army and Lisa would be there, too.

"I'll be there," I said.

Two days later, Granddad drove me to the airport. Before I opened the passenger side door, he stopped me with a request.

He looked me squarely in the eyes, which froze me to my seat. "Would you tell her for me that I didn't know?" he asked. I was self-conscious under his direct gaze, certain I would somehow fumble. "Tell her that I would have taken all of you—Mimi and I would have taken all of you—if we had known," he finished.

I promised I would tell her.

Rebekah Two

We gotta figure out what we're gonna call the new one," Jacob said. "Rebekah Two?"

"Big Rebecca and Little Rebekah?" Lisa offered.

"Nobody wants to be called Big anything," Peggy said.

It was the Friday night of Memorial Day weekend. Late. Jacob, Lisa, Peggy, and I were working our way through a bottle of Irish whiskey. Jacob was stateside for two weeks of leave from the Army; he'd return to Germany in a few days. Peggy had only consumed two ounces of actual liquor, but her voice was already thick and slow. My mother always had been a lightweight.

"How about Becca and *Re*-bekah?" I said. "You know, like that joke about Pete and Re-Peat?"

"Pete and Re-Peat sat on a fence . . ." Peggy said.

It was a joke Granddad told over the breakfast table. Jacob and Lisa had no idea what we were talking about. For a moment, Peggy and I were frozen in separate but similar pasts, replaying his voice our heads. *Pete and Re-Peat sat on a fence. Pete fell off and who was left?* Had Granddad kept repeating the lines until the child Peggy hollered, "I get it! I GET IT! You can STOP now!" like I had? Did she think the Becca and *Re*-bekah thing was funny like

I did, or did it remind her of our strange dual relation, mother-sister, sister-daughter? Another echo, another record skipping.

"We only got one of 'em here this time," Jacob said. "We can figure it out later."

Becca hadn't made the trip. She said she had to work.

Peggy yawned at the head of the table. "Let's toast before I go to bed," she said. "I'll teach you my favorite one."

We raised our glasses and she intoned:

May those that love us, love us
And those that don't, may God turn their hearts.
If He cannot turn their hearts, may He turn their ankles,
So we will know them by their limping.

We clinked glasses and sipped. The fiery burn of the alcohol seemed the perfect companion to the searing bitterness of the words. It fit us perfectly. Jacob poured a portion of whiskey in a shot glass that he set in front of an empty chair. "For Becca," he intoned, "absent but not forgotten!"

We drank to that. We found drinking could help in the lead-up to a reunion. It kept the doubts at bay, lent the thing a party atmosphere. In my case, the booze calmed the waves of shakiness that could sometimes overtake me. This was my third reunion. I was developing strategies to make it through the thing. I worried that this form of self-medication wasn't exactly healthy, but I needed it.

After Peggy went to bed, my siblings and I moved to the living room to sit in softer chairs. Lisa curled, catlike, into a corner of the love seat and I sat beside her. Jacob groaned as he stretched into the full length of the sofa. I hadn't been in this room since the day I met Lisa. Every visible inch of wall space in the place was now covered in photographs of my siblings and me. We surveyed the framed faces staring back at us.

"It's like her way of never letting us go again," Lisa whispered.

Mixed among the faces we knew, there was a photo of Meghan and Lesley, the youngest two sisters, whom none of us had met yet. Their mother sent this picture to Peggy in a Christmas card. Meghan, the older sister, was dark like me. Lesley was blue-eyed and light-haired like Becca and Lisa. If I squinted, it could have been a photograph of me and Becca at the same ages. It was surreal to look at that photo and see myself in it, knowing that these girls had no idea that we existed, that we were waiting for them.

Lisa followed my gaze.

"You ever think you'd be a big sister?" I asked.

"Hell, no," Lisa said. "I didn't know about the younger ones until I met you."

It was after two in the morning when Jacob passed out on the sofa. Lisa and I retired to the guestroom.

Jacob and Lisa had both grown up in Jersey and shared a generational and geographical vocabulary. They drank coffees from Wawa and went down the shore in summertime. They knew the names of the Phillies and Eagles starting lineups, how to drive on snowy roads. Because he was close by, Jacob had been able to attend Lisa's school plays and high school graduation. A month into her freshman year of college, Lisa got in a fight with her boyfriend in the middle of the night, and Jacob was the person she called to come help. He'd been between training rotations stateside, before the Army shipped him out to Germany. He drove over an hour to pick her up and they sat in the booth of a twenty-four-hour diner until she calmed down.

Unlike Lisa and Jacob, Lisa and I weren't integrated into one another's lives outside the world of our reunions. My friends didn't know about her; hers didn't know about me. But we talked. We had monthly marathon phone calls, sent emails, and on nights like tonight, when we were drunk on whiskey and proximity, Lisa and I crawled into the same bed and whispered to one another until the sun came up.

It was clear that my sister had been a popular girl in high school; she was skilled at making a person feel privileged to be her confidante. Lisa was cliquish and conspiratorial in an intoxicating way when she whispered about her dreams for the future and hearts that she had—regrettably—broken in her long career as a pretty girl. She craved the family stories that none of the adults wanted to tell, and I was happy to share them. The ones about Joan and Mac, schizophrenia and loaded guns, and the real reason Jacob left Oklahoma. She was a beautiful audience, absorbing each saga with wide eyes, saying, *What happened next?* and *Ohmygod*, at the perfect moments, as if I'd written the lines for her myself.

Delight rose off her like smoke from a campfire when she spoke about her plans to leave college and move to Orlando to pursue a singing career. Her energy ebbed only when she mentioned her father, how he wanted her to finish school first. For the briefest moment, my bubbly sister grew quiet. She hadn't yet told him of her intentions. "He won't be happy about it," she said. Though her mother, it seemed, was enthusiastic about anything Lisa wanted to do. I wondered why Orlando and not New York. Lisa said something about the home base of the pop music industry and the weather in Florida, but all I could think was that it was far away from all of her family, biological and adopted.

We were out of bed as soon as it was reasonable to make a cup of coffee. We tiptoed through the living room, where Jacob still slumbered, stopping to cover any bit of skin that stuck out from his blanket in a layer of Post-it notes. He looked like a lizard covered in yellow scales. Then Lisa and I hurried into the kitchen before we laughed and roused him. I had just started brewing the coffee when we heard paper crinkle and hit the wood floor with a *pfft*.

"You think you're real fuckin' cute, huh?" Jacob called grogily through the doorway.

I didn't want to wake Peggy yet. Post-reunion with Lisa, Peggy had asked me if I thought my newly rediscovered sister was angry with her. "I wouldn't blame her if she was," Peggy hurried to say. Lisa didn't say anything about it, I told Peggy. She hadn't, then, but months after the reunion, during a phone call, Lisa said, "Angry isn't the word. It's more skeptical. Peggy talks like she didn't have anything to do with giving us up, like she was a victim."

Lisa never knew what Peggy was like before all this. My sister didn't see that the act of giving up her children had altered the mother I had. We could never get that woman back. She had been buried under the weight of the things she'd lost. I never found the words to articulate this to my sister. Maybe that was okay. Lisa's relationship with Peggy was separate from my own; the woman she knew was a completely different person.

So today I let Peggy sleep. And I cooked pancakes. We finished the coffee and made a fresh pot.

After breakfast, the apartment filled with the spruce and cedar scent of Jacob's shaving cream. Lisa and I primped in the same mirror in the guest bedroom, littering the top of the dresser with flatirons and lipsticks. Becca had never been interested in feminine things; she always turned to me to do something with her hair or apply her makeup for a rare date. But Lisa offered to style the back of my hair, asked could she borrow my lip gloss.

This was what we would have been like. This was how it would feel to have a sister whose sweaters I could borrow, who would wear my earrings and tell me if I put on too much eyeliner. We would have fought over who, in fact, had bought that buttery leather jacket, our tempers raising the same high color to our cheeks. I could see it as we gazed into the same mirror. Another life was contained in our matching faces, in which we were safe fighting and hating and forgiving one another because the force of our affection was great enough to withstand anything.

The doorbell rang. Lisa and I dropped lip balms and mascara tubes on the dresser and closed the bedroom door to the disarray of half-unpacked suitcases and toiletries strewn over the furniture. Our sister was here.

The apartment floors creaked under the weight of seven pairs of feet as Peggy, Jacob, Lisa, and I joined Rebekah and her parents in the living room. The small room squeezed us together, forced us to brush shoulders and stare into each other's eyes. Rebekah was five feet tall, with brown bangs sweeping across her forehead. Brown eyes, fair skin, delicate features. She was the spitting image of Peggy's mother, Joan, right down to the crooked front incisor.

Her parents hovered in the doorway between the kitchen and the living room. It hadn't occurred to me that this sister wouldn't come alone. She was nineteen, after all; old enough for autonomy. Her mother was slender, with short red hair, and her father rotund and quiet. They shared a wide-eyed glance when they noticed a photograph of their daughter on Peggy's wall.

I smiled at them as I introduced myself; hoped that my voice sounded warm. My sister's parents stayed tense and tight-lipped; their hands were cold. They watched their little girl plop onto the love seat with Peggy and spread a photo album across their laps. An act that seemed to sting in its simplicity. These parents had come along as a security blanket, and now they were discarded as their daughter gazed deeply into photos of previously unknown ancestors who looked like her.

Jacob, Lisa, and I squeezed onto the facing sofa. Rebekah's parents hovered in the doorway, blinking. I would have understood their discomfort as apprehension and nerves, but I was hung up on the fact that I seemed to be a part of the thing they feared. My skin prickled. I didn't like being appraised like that by strangers.

Thankfully they didn't stay long, and after a couple of hours Peggy left, too. She hadn't been able to get the day off work on such short notice. So Jacob, Lisa, Rebekah, and I were alone in the living room, surrounded by photos of our separate childhoods. We were all visitors here, waiting for a tour guide to point us in the right direction. Lisa was the first one to offer a plan.

"Let's go into Philly," she said, flipping her hair over her shoulder.

Tom let us take his convertible; he was working until late in the evening and wouldn't need it. When my siblings and I were together, we got whatever we wanted. Jacob slid in the driver's seat and we three girls crammed in the back. We put the top down and turned the radio up. The voice of a pop singer spelling the word *BANANAS* thumped through the speakers. I started giggling uncontrollably. The lack of sleep caught up to me. Lisa stared at me and started laughing, too.

"I hate this song!" I said when I caught my breath.

"This song is BANANAS," Lisa agreed.

"You're BANANAS," Jacob hollered from the driver's seat.

"No, we're BANANAS," Lisa said.

She was right. The four of us in a yellow convertible driving into Philadelphia on Memorial Day weekend was bananas. It was absurd. It was wonderful and odd. The bubble that I recalled from my first meeting with Lisa began to slowly form around us. The sun felt like butter on my bare shoulders, the radio blared top 40 hits that we all knew, and for a moment we were just kids, soaking in a beautiful summer day. We drove forward. We insisted that the force of our will would eventually make this day happen the way we needed it to. We needed our fix, the feeling that we were a world unto ourselves; that we shared things that belonged only to us. That the universe would hand us the things we wanted because we had lost so much and the scales needed to be balanced. But something was off. We shot past cars headed the opposite direction from us; Philadelphians were headed out of the city and toward the Jersey Shore. We were driving against the tide. Rebekah squinted, silently, beneath the shelf of her bangs. The bubble was forming, but she was on the outside of it.

Through the whipping wind and my caffeine haze, I tried to focus on this new sister. It seemed imperative that I draw her in with the rest of us. "You've heard our story," I said. "Tell us yours."

Rebekah's face went pale. The wind shattered her voice and sent it a million directions.

She had been home-schooled until she started college the previous fall. "That's why I started my blog," she shouted at me, "to connect with other home-school kids." She had attended a Christian school until third grade, when the romantic overtures of a teacher caused Rebekah's mom to pull her out. "He basically tried to kiss my mom a couple of times and she was totally freaked."

Rebekah laughed so it would seem offhand. It didn't seem off-hand. "I wanted to be home-schooled, though," she insisted. Strangers were not her favorite thing. I understood that feeling.

Lisa nodded on the other side of the backseat, but I don't think she caught more than a few words. She leaned over the passenger seat and turned the radio up.

Over the Walt Whitman Bridge Rebekah told me that her dad was "basically agoraphobic, you know, afraid of the outside world." Her stories were full of friends she had never met in person. Her boyfriend, in fact, was one of these people. The boy was a home-school student in Oregon, so their interactions were primarily over the phone. They had planned visits many times, but something always fell through. So though they had "dated" for over a year, Rebekah at nineteen still hadn't had her first kiss.

Rebekah's hands fluttered like a couple of birds as she talked. She was electric with nerves. Something about her jitters forced me to be calm in a way that I was normally incapable of. I could see the blood pumping up the veins in her neck. She was two baby steps away from a full-scale panic attack. Pointing this out could possibly make it worse, I knew. Admitting that I knew anything about panic attacks would also destroy my carefully curated big-sister act. I wanted to pull Rebekah onto my lap and absorb the nervous shakes out of her. But she wasn't a baby, and we were still relatively unknown to one another.

I reached out for one of Rebekah's baby-bird hands, to still her if I could. I willed the calmness I felt toward her, imagining some-thing akin to squeezing toothpaste out of a tube. If I had to will a connection, I would; I had always been the diligent sister, the diligent daughter. I had to find something we shared. Something that was us, not everyone. Something other than panic. Anxious

Mary was not the person I was during a reunion. Anxious Mary was the girl in my other life. I didn't want her to show up and ruin what should be an amazing day. We would have beautiful memories of today if it killed me.

"You have piano hands," I said, "do you play?"

"I did for a while. When I was little. But not so much recently." Rebekah's hands were like mine—long tapered fingers, wide flat palms, tiny wrists. Hands designed to play instruments, or dance ballet, hands that "make it impossible to wear bracelets," we said in unison. This sister, I thought, was the one I had expected the first Rebecca to be, all those years ago in Camden. My echo, my shadow. I wasn't wrong to think that she was out there. I'd just had them in the wrong order.

Jacob parked off of South Street in Philadelphia, and we walked through the Italian Market. The scent of cooking sausages and grilled green peppers surrounded us. None of the strangers on the street gave us a second glance. When we stopped for dinner at a café, Rebekah kept her elbows in, carved up perfect bites. If crumbs fell on the table, she immediately tucked them into her napkin. It was a tense, studied way of eating. She noticed me watching her.

She giggled. "When I was little, I couldn't eat at the same time as my dad because the crumbs would send him into a meltdown." And she flipped her hair over her shoulder. In an eerie repeat of the precise way Lisa had performed the same gesture in Peggy's apartment. I thought I had invented that style of mimicry when I was a teenager. Seeing my little sister perform the same adaptation chilled me.

After dinner we learned that Rebekah had never smoked a cigarette or tasted alcohol. "Just hang out with us for a while," Lisa said.

Jacob and Lisa walked ahead, caught up in their own conversations about parties and people they knew that Rebekah and I didn't.

I fell into step with Rebekah, who continued to chatter about everything she could think to tell me about herself. Dances with the swing club at her small Christian college in rural Pennsylvania, her plan to study abroad the next year, favorite bands, and books she'd read. She was majoring in English, like I had.

I was suddenly self-conscious about the way Lisa recounted the DUI she got last year ("So, I *had* been drinking, but no way I ran that stop sign. Cop was a total liar"), and the casual way I discussed Becca's recreational activities. "I'm pretty sure she's growing magic mushrooms in her kitchen," I had said on the drive, and we all laughed and shook our heads. I thought I was so clever. We needed to downshift, be gentler. Talk about movies and the weather; tell the story about Granddad's father and the potato salad fiasco. Rebecca would like that one, I thought.

When we returned to Peggy's, Lisa and Jacob continued their howling conversation about several times they had escaped death or public mortification. Their voices were like a leaf blower taking over the entire room. Rebekah sat politely at the other end of the table, her hands folded in her lap, watching them like a starved puppy watching a pork chop. Her parents would be back to collect her soon.

Unlike the previous reunion, today I saw the end before it came. I was fully aware of the impending comedown. I felt the universe slip way. My powers of command over the world started to wane. In a moment I would no longer feel like I could stop traffic with a smile. Jacob's and Lisa's voices would lose their brightness, their laughter would quiet. The vibrant colors of the world would start to run and bleed and everything would be covered in dust again. It would happen in an instant; we would go from in-reunion to post-reunion. We would crash.

The trip flashed before my eyes like a near-death experience: Rebekah's shaking hands. My mushroom story; Lisa's DUI; the frightened-rabbit look in Rebekah's eyes. My anxiety; her anxiety; Peggy's tiny apartment. Time, ticking away. It was over. And it hadn't been that good to begin with. My stomach crept toward my throat.

I grabbed four beers from the fridge and placed them in the middle of the kitchen table. Rebekah grabbed one without hesitation. It wasn't a test so much as it was an answer to a question that I couldn't ask out loud. Rebekah wanted to be one of us. I wanted her to be one of us, too. But I also wanted to protect her along the way if I could.

We raised our glasses and bottles around the kitchen table and Jacob said:

May those that love us, love us . . .

For the last thirty minutes that we had together, Rebekah, Lisa, and I listened to Jacob's stories about Germany; how he had driven on the Autobahn ("It's scary as hell, but awesome") and attended beer festivals and strawberry festivals ("Germans got festivals for any kind of food. They friggin' love festivals"). In that half an hour, time flew by. But for a moment we were together, laughing about the same things; it was a shiny button on an otherwise strange day.

Rebekah's parents didn't come to the door; they called from the driveway and we walked her down to their waiting sedan. Her father eyeballed us through his rolled-up window as if he were on a wilderness adventure and we were a bunch of wild boars circling his Honda. As they pulled into the street, Rebekah kept her eyes on us through the rear window of the car. I waved until I was sure she couldn't see me anymore.

The look on her father's face touched something primal in me. He didn't seem to like me, so I decided I didn't like him right back. It was a response that had been grafted onto my bones as a child: that weak people get hurt and strong people get even.

Besides the little I remembered about meeting them when I was a child, I never gave much thought to my sisters' parents, but now they were becoming a confounding factor I could not ignore.

I had always told myself that adoption was a kind of triple-win scenario—birth families relieve the pressure of a child they are unable to care for, adoptive families gain a much wanted child, child gains a stable, loving family—but I was beginning to see that there was a flipside. There can be no winners without losers. So in a triple-win, there must be a related triple-loss. Once adoption was on the table, everyone has already lost—lineage, origin, the vision of the future lives they thought they would live—and all our losses were attached to someone else's gain in an endless, confusing loop.

Rebekah's father did not steal my sister from me anymore than I planned to steal his daughter from him. But my regaining my sister was directly related to the anguish he felt at being left behind. And my sadness at having lived this far in my life without Rebekah was linked to his having raised her in the first place. So my face became the image he attached his pain to. And his was the symbol for my grief.

On my return flight to Oklahoma, I nursed an angry hurt that Becca hadn't made it to this reunion. If she knew anything well, it was how to handle a hard time coming down from a bad trip.

———

OKLAHOMA CITY was exactly as I had left it. Mimi still bruised like a peach and Granddad still sang "Oh! How I Hate to Get Up in the Morning" in the morning. After this reunion, though, I couldn't sleep. I'd pass out for an hour a night, but never more.

During those long, sleepless hours I stalked Rebekah's blog. The things she wrote were so intense that I wanted both to look away and wallow in them. I wished she had someone to talk to, someone who might advise her that someday she might regret writing these things for strangers to see. But on the other hand, I loved that it allowed me to look into her mind. Rebekah wrote that since she'd experienced "what a true family felt like," she'd grown angry over the things that were missing from her extended adoptive family. Her father's relatives had never really accepted her as a full-blooded family member. To them Rebekah always had an asterisk. She was their Adopted* granddaughter, Adopted* niece.

Rebekah wrote that she felt like a tapestry of qualities that she inherited from her biological family and her adoptive family; she was terrified of being too much of either of them. She didn't want to be anxious to the point of paralysis like her adoptive father, nor dreamy to the point of failure like her birth father, Michael (whom she'd met on a subsequent solo trip). She'd always felt a void in her life, she said, and after meeting us she knew what it was: it was us. She sensed a kinship with me and Jacob and Lisa, but because of her father's ailments she felt obligated to remain quiet to avoid upsetting him. She wrote that she didn't know what she was supposed to feel or what she was allowed to feel; she wasn't sure she was entitled to feel anything.

Hardest to read of all of it were the stories she told about her father. Rebekah blamed herself for his anxiety. She said, now, that she walked on eggshells in social situations because growing up with her father had ingrained the habit. Seeing those words broke my heart afresh. The thoughts Rebekah recorded on her blog were echoes of the ones I had recorded in the canvas journals locked in my childhood closet. We had the same voice, the same thoughts, the same way of feeling guilty for everything that happened to us. I was relieved to find a spiritual kinship in this sister, but my gut thumped with the knowledge that I had developed all of the characteristics we shared as a result of trauma, which meant she had, too.

That wasn't how it was supposed to happen. Wasn't there an implied deal in adoption; that the adoptive parents would take better care of a child than her biological family could? Rebekah was supposed to be stronger, more confident, smarter, better adjusted, more graceful, charming, and educated than I was, wasn't she?

The only things I remember Peggy asking for was that my sisters' new parents promise to send the girls to college and that they allow the girls to search for us. Those were the only unbending demands she'd made. Where they had once seemed hopeful, they now seemed tragically naïve.

After our reunion, Rebekah called me every couple of weeks. In January, she confided that she'd argued with her father about her plans to see Peggy and Jacob when she was home from school over the holidays. Her father told Rebekah that as long as she was living in his house she could never see "those people" again. He didn't see what Rebekah was so upset about; it wasn't like we were her real family anyway.

Those words hit me like a truck: *real family*. They brought me back to a day when I was a kid and I had asked Peggy what the word *bastard* meant. She told me it meant "illegitimate, like not real." It had seemed like a toothless insult. But now I understood where the word had bite: If you are not real, you can be dismissed, erased, forgotten. It means that you don't matter.

Rebekah fought with her father through Christmas. She spent Christmas Eve by herself in her childhood bedroom, watching reruns of *Friends*. Then she drove herself to a parking lot and cried for an hour, listening to that stupid banana song on repeat.

Join the Club

Peggy met my third lost sister, Meghan, in the clearance aisle of the department store where she worked. It was August, three months after we'd reunited with Rebekah. Peggy was pacing the store with a sticker gun in her hand when Meghan appeared with her mother. They lived in the same town and Peggy frequently saw them at the store, usually with Meghan's little sister and the last of our lost siblings, Lesley, in tow.

Meghan and Lesley were the last of our set of seven, born two years apart. Like Becca and me, they were adopted by the same parents and grew up together. But in all the years that they shopped at that southern New Jersey store they didn't know that the woman in the red polo shirt was their birth mother. She was some lady their mother chatted with on the way to the toy aisles. They probably never noted Peggy's features to the point that they could pick her out of a lineup.

On this particular August afternoon, it was just Meghan and her mom. It was the end of summer, when the patio furniture displays faded into back-to-school season. The shelves overflowed with notebooks and extra-long sheet sets. The ends of the aisles were claimed by die-cut pencils shouting, A+ PRICES and SCHOOL COOL!

From the edge of the main thoroughfare Meghan's mother waved to Peggy as she had many times over the years. Peggy approached with the standard manual-issue verbiage: "Can I help you find something?" But rather than asking about ChapStick or lunch boxes, the other mother said, "Well, Meghan, here she is. This is your biological mother."

The truth fell between them like a freshly shot bird dropping from the sky. Peggy had four more hours in her shift. I imagine the fluorescent light made her skin green and her red work shirt brought out the rosacea in her cheeks in a way that she hated. She had to rest her sticker gun against her hip to shake Meghan's hand.

"She has my phone number. She knows where I live," Peggy told me on the phone later that night. "Why would she do it that way?"

We told one another that we didn't understand it, that we couldn't wrap our minds around the strange woman's behavior. But I suspected that she was afraid of us, like Rebekah's father had been. That she wanted to diminish Peggy and look superior by comparison. I couldn't say it out loud. If Peggy was thinking the same thing, I didn't want to reinforce it.

I FLEW to New Jersey the week before Christmas for the proper reunion. Winter weather in the Midwest kept me grounded in Oklahoma City until after dark.

When I finally walked into the baggage claim at Newark Airport after midnight, I was greeted with a *whoop*. Jacob, Becca, Lisa, Rebekah, and Meghan bounced against one another. No one was in a holiday mood but the six of us; the slog of winter travel delays and lost baggage made the other travelers silent background extras in our scene. This was our airport, our stage, our story.

I'd never thought that Becca and I looked alike. Not even related. My features came from our grandmothers. Becca took after Granddad and Peggy. We looked as different as two siblings could. Meghan, however, had my nose and mouth, with Becca's cheeks and chin. She was the missing link between us. She had Jacob's chocolate-brown eyes, long brown hair like me and Little Rebekah, with Becca's high, round cheeks. She had Lisa's social ease and popular girl manner.

Jacob grabbed my luggage. He'd finished his assignment in Germany and was enjoying a month stateside before his first tour in Afghanistan. He'd married an American girl, a Texan named Katy, whom he'd met on post. They'd had a small ceremony in Germany and honeymooned in Italy. It was a rushed affair with no time for invitations. Jacob had called Peggy to tell her the news the day before the wedding and I found about it second-hand. Jacob and Katy planned to have a "real wedding" stateside after Jacob came back from his tour in Afghanistan.

"The wife is back at Ma's, sleeping. You'll meet her tomor-row," my brother told me through a sloppy grin. Katy was five months pregnant and needed her rest. It was surreal to think that Jacob was going to be a father in mere months. We hadn't even met all the sisters yet, our set was not yet complete, and already my brother was starting his own family.

I draped my arm over Meghan's shoulder and she wrapped her arm around my waist as we walked to the car. Maybe because she'd had a day of getting to know everyone already, or maybe because I was accustomed to these reunions by now, Meghan seemed immediately familiar.

"Mary gets shotgun, and I don't wanna hear any whining," Jacob barked when we reached the parking garage.

There weren't enough seat belts for everyone in the backseat. Rebekah sat on Becca's lap. We were unaccustomed to planning for a number of us. Jacob had to turn on the air-conditioning because the heat of our bodies and breath fogged the windows to the point that he couldn't see in any direction. As he pulled onto the highway it started to snow.

"I gotta apologize for my mom," Meghan said. She spoke with a slight lisp; it gave her a charming underdog quality.

I looked over to Jacob in the front seat. I wasn't going to pick up that live wire. Neither was he.

"That was unbelievably bitchy," Lisa said.

We drove into a tunnel of snow.

"Mary, you should have been here last night," Becca said. Lisa, Rebekah, and Meghan groaned their agreement.

"I thought we weren't gonna tell her about that!" Jacob giggled. "I'm never trusting you punks with anything."

My siblings talked in a hurry to catch me up. Their voices teased and gamboled and leapt; they piled on top of one another in one breathless mountain.

They'd spent the night before in Peggy and Tom's kitchen
Playing this drinking game,
"With cards"
A circle of death
"No, King's Cup, we call it King's Cup"
"It's the same thing"
ANYWAY

They played this game and
"Lisa made this rule that no one could remember"
Because they had been drinking
And then they drank more
"So much"
And "Re-bekah threw UP in the bathroom"
And "Becca passed OUT"
And "Jacob dropped her head on the hardwood floor when he tried to lift her onto the sofa in the living room"
"It *bounced*"
And the other sisters gasped
And he said
"IT'S A PROCESS"
Their howls of laughter escaped through the seams of the car, into the night air.

Everyone woke up this morning with matching hangovers.

"It's a good thing your flight was delayed," Jacob said. "We were all still drunk until an hour ago."

At our last reunion I had accepted a nip of booze as an elixir that was an integral part of the developing relationship with my sisters; it eased our jitters, gave us something to do with our hands. But it was easy to overdo it. Maybe in the future it would be better if we all took up knitting.

"If you'd been here you would have kept us in line," Becca said, as if she could read my mind.

"I don't know about that . . ." I demurred; I didn't want a reputation as a killjoy.

"You know you would've," Jacob said. "It's what you do. Mother Mary."

It was after one in the morning when we reached the apartment. Peggy and Tom and Jacob's new wife were asleep. So we went to a twenty-four-hour diner, where six cups of coffee would pay the rent on a corner booth for a few hours.

Diners always reminded me of the days I lost my sisters. The smell of coffee burning on a hot plate and peanut oil bubbling in a fryer brought me back to those days with Peggy, those ominous lunches. The suck of vinyl booths sticking to the back of my legs and the feel of bumpy gum topography beneath the linoleum tabletops were an inextricable part of my family mythology.

This diner was sparsely populated. The real holiday was days away. We ordered our coffees and an assortment of fried things—onion rings mixed with french fries and chicken fingers. After the delay and the flight and the drive I was ravenous.

"Lesley doesn't know that you guys exist yet," Meghan said. She took a deep breath. "I'm not allowed to tell her. Mom doesn't want to upset her. She's acting out a lot and being . . . unstable."

"Mary grew up with someone like that," Becca said, raising a self-referential eyebrow.

Since the last time I saw Becca, she'd met someone: a good Catholic girl whom she had followed to Minneapolis. My sister came out to me just before her move. In some ways it made perfect sense: No wonder she had raged against her life as a teenager, no wonder she felt out of place. No wonder she struggled more than I did in her adolescence. Becca was more clear-eyed than she had been in years. She'd gained ten pounds, filled in the hollows around her eyes and cheekbones. Tonight, Becca was the healthiest I'd seen her in years.

"I didn't know what adoption meant until I found my hospital bracelet in my parents' closet," Meghan continued. "It had Peggy's name on it and I asked my mom if that was what my name was supposed to be."

Lisa shook her head and braced herself against the table. "I'm sorry, that's just fucked. I mean . . . how could your parents lie your whole life?"

"I was eight or nine; it wasn't my whole life. And it wasn't totally a lie," Meghan said. She leaned back in the booth, digging for deeper memories. "My mom mentioned the word adoption when I was younger. I was five, I think. We were talking about where babies come from. I could tell she didn't like talking about it. She kept saying we'd talk about it when I was older. The day that I found the bracelet was the day I realized what the word adoption *meant*, you know?"

Rebekah nodded from the corner of the booth. "It had to be horrible to find out that way, though," she said.

With each subsequent reunion Rebekah had come out of her shell more. She had an incredible ear for indie bands that none of us had heard of; she'd begun deejaying at her college radio station. She sporadically mailed me mix CDs. When she turned her head to look at Meghan, I saw a dainty stud embedded in her left nostril. That was new.

"The weirdest part was when we were little," Meghan went on. "Lesley always said that she felt like she had a piece missing, like a hole inside that wasn't right. She sensed it the whole time. She's gonna shit when she finds out about all of you."

I was eager to meet Lesley and complete our set. I could see from the glint in my siblings' eyes that we all were. Just miles from this diner—a fifteen-minute drive—seventeen-year-old Lesley was asleep in her bed. The thought made my pulse race. We could go there right now. We sipped our coffee and considered patience.

Meghan was in the premed program at a rural Pennsylvania college. She planned to go directly into medical school and become an obstetrician. When she heard the college I had attended, she squealed.

"I applied there and didn't get in! Can you imagine if I had?"

"We would have just missed one another," I said. But she would have known people and places that knew me. Deeper digging revealed that she and Lesley had been in a summer martial arts class that Jacob had taught when they were kids. The realization of these near misses amazed all of us.

"I'm gonna be here the rest of my life. So you guys'll have to move back." Meghan gave me, Becca, and Jacob serious looks.

As soon as the statement was out of her mouth, it was the only thing I wanted to do. I could get a little apartment in South Jersey. We could meet once in a while for dinner. I wouldn't demand to spend actual holidays with the girls—that would be too much—but we could find days around holidays. We'd meet each other's friends and coworkers. We'd introduce one another as, *This is my little sister, this is my big sister.*

"What the hell happened with you guys?" Meghan asked bluntly.

Jacob and Becca groaned loudly.

"Newcomer's going straight for the jugular!" Jacob crowed.

Everyone looked at me. I was the only one who had been through all of it—who'd lived with Peggy and Michael, who'd stayed in Oklahoma when Jacob had left, who had been adopted alongside Becca. I'd pocketed the pieces of our story so I would be able to answer questions for my sisters when they returned, but now that I had the opportunity, I wasn't sure I wanted to burden them with the truth. What was the truest answer to that question, anyway? What had happened with Jacob, Becca, and me?

"Peggy and Michael were broke," was what I settled on. "When they divorced, neither one could afford to keep us and Peggy didn't want to split us up."

"But you did get split up," Lisa noted.

"I didn't like Oklahoma," Jacob said. "And it didn't like me, either."

"Why the hell did they keep having kids?" Meghan asked.

It was a question that I wanted an answer to myself.

"I don't know," I said. "They were good at having them, just not good at keeping them. You'd have to ask Peggy."

I knew that Peggy and Michael didn't believe in abortion. Birth control in general was a murkier area. When I received my first prescription birth control pills in college, I recognized the plastic clamshell setup because I'd seen one in Peggy's nightstand in Marigold Court. Either she wasn't conscientious, or she couldn't afford to get them consistently. Or she thought maybe having another baby would save her marriage, save the family she'd always wanted. But there was one thing I knew for sure; I'd heard my ex-father say it so many times.

"Michael thought it was God's will; that it was their duty to bring you girls into the world and give you to people who couldn't have children. It was his ministry." My sisters nodded into their coffee.

As a little girl I had accepted my sisters' births as facts. But with time to reflect, it was clear that they were the bombing campaign that my already fragile family was not strong enough to withstand. The girls around this table were people I loved, people I lost, and people whose existence had ripped my family apart. All of these things were true. None of these truths was strong enough to erase the others. It would be easier if one of them could.

———

MEGHAN EVENTUALLY had to go home. It was her Christmas break and her days were filled with family obligations. We made plans to meet again at Peggy's later that afternoon, if she could get away.

"I wish it could have been different," I said when Meghan hugged me goodbye.

"Yeah," she said. "Me, too."

By the time the rest of us made it back to Peggy and Tom's apartment the sun was already climbing up the sky and sleep seemed ludicrous. Jacob, Becca, Lisa, Rebekah, and I tried not to make any noise as we opened the door. Peggy was already awake, brewing a pot of coffee in the kitchen. The inviting smell of coffee and cinnamon wafted around her in her light blue pullover.

Her eyes lit up at the sight of the five of us slinking into the house after dawn. "It's all I ever wanted, for you all to find each other," she said. Then she grabbed my hands and rubbed them between hers, demanding to know how I'd come to New Jersey in December without gloves.

Quarter-Life Crisis

Meghan didn't make it back to college for the spring semester. She said she was just taking a break. A month after she dropped out, she drove the wrong way on a freeway and crashed into another driver. The mangled remains of both vehicles made the local papers.

It was incredible that she didn't die, that she didn't kill anybody. But then, my siblings and I seemed to be charmed that way; we were just lucky enough to live after we unluckily torpedoed our lives. Her parents got her a great lawyer and she managed to avoid jail time. But Meghan had to plead guilty to some things, so she would never be a doctor now. She would have to find another way to be.

If I was willing to admit it, there was a pattern of chaos developing in my younger sisters. Peggy had sent them away from us when they were born so they could have lives free from the strange warping force of our family, but the cruel joke was that all of my sisters slid into a downward spiral soon after they met us. Even after all these years we were still a liability.

When I met her for the first time, Becca was a whip-smart little girl who absorbed knowledge like a sponge. After her stint in New

Jersey she became a caterwauling ball of angst. She was searching and unsettled. Dropping out of college, getting into drugs.

Lisa, too, dropped out of college, and moved to Orlando, then Denver. She dated alcoholics and men who slapped her. Every few months my phone would ring at three in the morning with a drunk Lisa on the other end of the line sobbing. The reason behind her wails was never intelligible. What was clear, though, was that a stream of sadness had been turned on inside her like a water spigot and it needed to be released somehow. I cooed, *You're okay, you're okay*, and tried to stay awake until she was finished. We never spoke about those calls in the light of day.

Just after the New Year Peggy called to tell me that Rebekah was in the hospital after taking too many aspirin. When Rebekah told me about it herself a week later, she said she'd had a headache and she misread the label, silliest thing; the print is so small it's no wonder.

Even after I spoke to Rebekah, the story haunted me. How many aspirin would a person need to take to be hospitalized? Was it truly a case of a misread label or did she have a self-destructive force in her?

For as long as I could remember, I had carried a sense of dread with me. It was a feeling, low and constant, that there was a black hole at my core that would swallow me whole if I relaxed my guard. This was what my childhood desire to disappear into the wind had become. My need to keep that great void from crushing me was what prevented me from trusting my own instincts. It was in me, and I could not escape it; it was a flaw in my foundational fabric that would draw tribulation to me unless I was vigilant and good.

I wanted to believe that Rebekah did not share this trait. But I was starting to believe that the impulse that drew us together was the very thing that tore us apart.

Our reunions were a brush with another dimension; with the people we might have been. All people fantasize about mythical ways their lives could have been different; in their minds they finally walk down the road not taken and play out new chains of events. Part of growing up is realizing that it doesn't matter, in the end you would be the same person, as likely to have ended up where you are regardless of what choice you made. But for my sisters and me that sort of fantasizing is not ephemera. It is a complete alternate reality in which we had enough information to fill in the blanks. We saw the cracks we would have fallen through, the rooms where we would have slept, the woman who would have been our mother, the man who would have been our father. Maybe we loved them, hated them, or pitied them—either way, the emotions were real. The adoptions themselves suddenly seem arbitrary enough that they could easily never have happened. With a few minor changes of circumstance, we might not have become the people we know ourselves to be. Thoughts like that were enough to drive anyone to drink, swallow half a bottle of pills, run their car into oncoming traffic, date dangerous men.

It was only a matter of time before destruction found me, too. As I searched for a post-college plan for my life, each of my days became a repeat of the previous one: I temped in the legal department of a local bank, I administered Mimi's breathing treatment, I watched the news with Mimi and Granddad, and then I lay in bed until the sun came up. After the reunion with Meghan, I stopped sleeping.

After a few weeks without sleeping my digestive system shut down. Food went in, but nothing came out. A stabbing pain emanating from above my left hipbone was constant. In the mornings, I needed the hot steam from the shower before I could ease my body into standing.

I lived with a couple of septuagenarians; foods designed to keep a body "regular" were easy to come by. One night I ate half of box of apple crisp fiber wafers, leaning over the kitchen sink in the dark like some sort of fiber cookie junkie. But no amount of fibrous cookies, orange powders, or Smooth Move teas had any effect. After four weeks without sleeping, and three weeks without shitting, came the days when I threw up everything. The oatmeal and the coffee, the fibrous cookies consumed under the cover of night, the bile that couldn't exit through the twisted coiled cramping mass of my stomach and intestines. I was exhausted and couldn't sleep, hungry and couldn't eat. I left telltale empty bowls and coffee cups in the kitchen sink so Mimi and Granddad wouldn't notice.

When my breath reached the point where it could strip the paint off a car, I started taking a toothbrush to work. Every morning the cramps took longer to subside. I passed long afternoons at the legal department reception desk jamming pens into the fleshy parts of my hands to distract myself from the pain in my abdomen. Ink dots covered me like a pox. At two in the afternoon it was time for me to retire to the staff restroom and throw up my lunch. I hoped that if I behaved as if I were fine, then my ailment would pass.

One day the lead counsel at the bank nudged me after the morning meeting. "You're too smart to be a receptionist," he said. "Have you thought about law school?"

It seemed like a hint from the universe. Everyone I knew from college was in law school. Or they were working at investment firms. The advent of social media allowed me to see, in real time, the ways in which my peers—or, the people I wanted to be my peers—shot ahead of me on the professional ladder. I was living with my parents, temping in the legal department at a bank, and feeling like a loser. Next year the engagement photo bombardment would begin, then five years later the sonograms and baby pictures would appear on Facebook.

There was a word for members of my generation who—like me—failed to hit these milestones on schedule. The phrase *quarter-life crisis* was enjoying a vogue. I didn't like the term. It felt like a flimsy ailment for insubstantial people.

I left work that afternoon and drove aimlessly around Oklahoma City for hours. Trees, telephone poles, and stone fences brushed past my window. I toyed with the idea of pitching myself into one of these solid things, just so I could finally sleep. I imagined how the impact would feel. Cold steel would scrape against my bones, and those bones would stab into soft tissue. At every intersection, my mouth watered in anticipation.

I was crazed; I didn't know what horrors I was capable of. I wasn't even sure if I was awake or asleep. I guided the car into the parking lot of a bookstore. The nice one on the north side of Oklahoma City, the place where I met my math tutor in high school. Between Self-Help and Astrology I found what I was looking for: an LSAT test prep guide.

The store will be closing in fifteen minutes, the voice on the public address system announced.

With the book in my hand, I attempted to turn toward the cash registers but my weary feet were glued to the carpet. There were no barriers, no forces holding me down. I was heavy with lack of sleep, my stomach and intestines were hard as concrete and it was spreading to the rest of my body; I could not move. *Move*, I thought, willing the word down to my limbs. But my body defied me.

I was frozen in the middle of the aisle. The weight of the book in my hand was the only thing that told me that I was not dreaming. This was real. The hum of the fluorescent lights and the nutty aroma of coffee and scalded milk. The voice entreated, *Shoppers, please make your way to the cash registers with your purchases; the store is closing in ten minutes.*

I negotiated with my feet, pleaded with them to move along the carpet. *Move move move*, I thought. When they wouldn't, I glanced down at the taupe page in front of me and tried to appear absorbed. In the aisles around me, pant legs swished together as my fellow shoppers obediently hustled to the registers.

The lights were too bright. I closed my eyes. I felt sweat trickling down my spine, collecting in the waistband of my jeans. How long had my back been sweating? How long had my hands been sweating and why was it so hot in here and why were the lights so bright and strangers were laughing they could see me they *saw* me they *heard* me breathing and my heart thudded against my eardrums like it was trying to escape the immobile husk of me, *The store will be closing in three minutes*, the voice said. *Two minutes.* the voice said, and I told myself I was fine.

I whispered to myself, I'm fine.

Two minutes . . .

But the twang in the PA voice was gone. It was a new voice, a familiar voice, a voice that growled in the New Jersey accent that I had abandoned in second grade.

Pack it in, Pumpkin. Time to go.

It was talking to me.

Of course I am, genius. You're going nuts here.

It wasn't real. It couldn't be real. I closed my eyes tighter, chanted faster. I'mfineI'mfineI'mfineI'mfineI'mfine.

You're so full of shit. Literally. You're nowhere close to fine.

I'm fine.

You're leaving empty bowls in the sink at Mimi and Granddad's house.

They have enough to worry about.

Sugar, somebody needs to worry about you.

No, they don't.

You don't want them to really know you. Cuz if they really knew you they'd think they failed.

They know me. They're my . . . parents.

On paper . . .

Leave me alone. You aren't real!

Yeah, I am. You know. On some level, you've always known. That feeling, low and constant, that something was coming for you? You knew that was me.

I didn't think it would be like this. I thought that when you came for me it would be quick and final. Like a car accident, or a tornado, or cancer. Not a literal shit-storm.

I had to get your attention, Pumpkin.

Don't call me that.

Reminds you of who we really are, don't it?

I am not you.

Let it out; you're not hurting my feelings.

What do you want?

I want my turn. These last few years would have been a lot more fun if I were running things.

Well, you weren't.

Neither were you. You've never done a single thing that somebody didn't choose for you. There's no mystery why you're holding that book right now.

Sometimes I followed the advice of people who . . . knew better than me.

You did more than that; you let 'em call all the shots.

Maybe I did.

And are you happy with that?

I was until you started talking to me.

Bullshit. You've been miserable your whole life.

I haven't been miserable; I've been busy—

Busy?

Yeah, busy, sticking to the plan.

What plan? It's been one foot in front of the other for you since you were four. You only looked up long enough for someone to pat you on the head and point you in the next direction. You couldn't follow the same path again, step-for-step, if you tried.

Yes, I could.

You went along with everyone else's plans for you ever since you let Mimi and Granddad adopt you.

I didn't let them adopt me; I chose to be adopted.

That's not what I remember. I remember wanting to be back home, in New Jersey, with my mother. I remember being afraid all the time, being scared of Granddad after Jacob left, I remember being so homesick I thought I could die.

Do you remember wanting to eat every day? Wanting to have electricity? Wanting to go to school? Because I do. Does that make me a horrible person? Is it a crime to want to be around grown-ups who know how to take care of things, who show up on time to pick you up from dance recitals and school and sleepovers? Who are there every single day? I remember wanting to stay with my sister. I remember not wanting to end up a high school dropout, or in jail. Is that where you're talking to me from? Fucking jail?

No, I'm talking to you from the test prep aisle of the bookstore, because that's where you're standing holding a goddamn LSAT book!

Stop it.

No, you stop it! Put the book down. PUT THE FUCKING BOOK DOWN AND LOOK AT YOURSELF.

I don't want to . . .

So what do you want?

What do you want me to say?

I want YOU to WANT something for once. Something that nobody told you to want.

I want. I do. Want things.

Like what, princess?

I want something that will make this all worth it; I want the good stuff. I'm ready for the goddamn silver lining. I want to have sisters who live down the street, I want a family; I want a mother to call when I need to know the right temperature to cook a goddamn chicken. I want Sunday suppers and summer barbecues at lake houses. I want to stop second-guessing every tiny detail of every single day, every word that comes out of my mouth. I want to be brave. I want to jump without looking down all the time. I want to be able to watch a TV show without seeing things that remind me about my sisters, about the could-have-been family. I want us to push tables together in restaurants so we all fit, I want to fill benches and rows of bleachers with us, I want the world to make room. I want to laugh too loud and make people wish they were us. I want them to feel it. Those perfect families, those perfect packages, those smug titles for everyone—mother father sister brother, step-this and half-that. They all have words for what they are. And we don't. I want that.

One minute . . . The bookstore will be closing in one minute . . .

What?

What do you want to do with your life?

I don't know . . . What do you want to do?

I asked you first.

"Excuse me, miss, we're closed now."

There was a hand on my arm. A store clerk with thick glasses stared back at me.

"Are you all right?"

He touched my arm again in that overly familiar way that people of the plains have, believing, as they seem to, that they could never offend someone.

I didn't like people touching me. That simple thought was pure motivation and I moved my arm away. The book landed with a *thwap* on the floor and I turned on my heel and I left. *I am fine*, I said, and I left the book on the floor and the clerk in the aisle and I was gone. I walked until I felt the parking lot crunch beneath my feet. I leaned against my car and sucked in the night air in giant gulps.

I knew I wasn't going to sleep that night, but the act of lying in bed for a few hours soothed me. In the dark, I wondered if my spell in the bookstore was what it had been like for my grandmother Joan. Was this how the schizophrenia that led her to desert Peggy began? Was this what it was like for her when she heard the voices that told her to send her daughter away? Had I finally lost my mind?

I decided that the difference between Joan and me was that I realized I had a hallucination. I also realized that it must have been brought on by lack of sleep. It was a waking dream, which made some sense. My body wasn't sleeping, but my mind was still dreaming. Right? Of course. Obviously.

By 8:21 the next morning, I was back in my car wearing smart slacks and a silk blouse. I gulped from a mug of coffee. The caffeine couldn't have helped the insomnia, but it was the only thing that allowed me to function during daylight hours. I sat in the parking lot outside the bank building. I watched the clock on my cell phone creep closer to 8:30.

8:23—The phone was the exact phone that my best friend from high school chose before me. From the deep knot in my stomach, I heard, *You can't even pick out your own phone.* I grew nauseous. I pushed the car door open, but my legs refused to step onto the asphalt.

8:25—I had five minutes to walk through the lobby, take the elevator to the fifth floor, make the coffee, and be in the morning meeting.

8:27—The clock on my cell phone blinked. My hands wouldn't move.

8:29—If I sprinted from my car, through the lobby, and up the elevator to the fifth floor, I'd still be late for work.

I *was* late for work.

I'd never been late for work in my life.

8:30—I should have been at my desk, saying things like, *Good morning, sir*, and *The weather's getting chilly, don't you think?* But I wasn't. I was still in my car, in the parking lot, a hundred yards from my desk, and I wasn't going anywhere.

8:32—I was, officially, brazenly, late for work.

Fuck it.

I pulled the car door closed. I pinned my eyes wide and drove. I drove until I reached a doctor's office.

In my family, help came from a doctor or a priest. Ailments of the body went to the doctor; plagues of the mind and spirit were the purview of the priest. If neither of them could help you, then you didn't have a problem and you had to get over it.

The only available doctor was a friendly blond woman, a pediatrician. All the grown-up doctors were booked solid.

The pediatrician clicked her pen. She opened my chart and read back the list of symptoms I told the receptionist when I'd arrived at the front desk.

You're here for . . .

Insomnia.

And . . . chronic constipation?

I cringed.

Yeah. And other digestive stuff.

Vomiting? Reflux? Cramping?

Yes. Yes. Yes. All of those.

Fever?

No.

How long since you slept?

Three weeks. No. Four.

Lay back on the table, please.

She dug her fingers into my stomach. I concentrated on my breath. I didn't like people touching my body. I didn't even like *me* touching my body. Putting contact lenses in my own eyes was necessary for the sake of vanity, and even that small bit of business took me months to execute when I got the things in eighth grade. I concentrated on the ceiling tiles and shivered with humiliation.

We're gonna need an X-ray.

I put on a paper gown. A technician took three pictures of my viscera. A nurse filled four vials with my blood. I filled one cup with my urine. I waited. There were two missed calls on my cell phone from the temp agency. The pediatrician returned.

There were no signs of Crohn's, celiac. No obstructions.

She held the black and bluish film where I could see it. My softest places, twisted and knotted, collapsed in on themselves like bridges and tunnels ravaged by a storm.

You're all knotted up.

That's what it looks like.

These things are sometimes psychosomatic. Which means that—

It means it's all in my head.

That doesn't make it less real.

The pediatrician was earnest now.

How old are you?

Twenty-three.

She nodded.

Have you ever heard of a "quarter-life crisis"?

I imagined slapping her pert pink cheek.

You're too young to be so stressed out! Go for a jog! Hang out with your friends. Go to a football game!

She squeezed my knee and grinned into my face.

This should give you a little kick-start.

The pediatrician handed me a prescription slip.

It's a stimulant to get your insides moving.

She squeezed her hands closed, fingers over palms, like the way a person waves to a baby, to illustrate for me.

And this . . .

She jiggled a brown paper bag.

. . . this should give you a li'l boost.

The bag was filled with sample packs for Effexor.

It's an antidepressant. Take one of those packs a day. Should last you a month. If you're still blocked up after that . . . we'll have to get more aggressive.

I DIDN'T want to think what "more aggressive" would look like.

I was glad to have pills. Pills were a sign that I had a real problem, not an imagined one. I saw the doctor. She gave me pills. Therefore, I was ill. I filled my prescription and drove to the house on Forty-fourth Street. Mimi was napping; she was only awake for a few hours at a time now. Granddad was in the living room, eating the lunch he'd eaten for ten years—a red delicious apple, a handful of pretzels, and a diet Dr Pepper.

"I'm sick," I said when I passed him. "I have pills." I raised the bags for him to see. He looked concerned, asked if there was anything he could do, but I waved him off. I was taking care of it.

I took my pills and lay down in the guest bedroom. The drugs competed with one another to control my body. The antidepressant covered my senses in a nonstick coating, while the stimulant liquefied my insides. Outside, I was Teflon and inside, I effervesced. It was not pleasant and not unpleasant. I stared at the drop ceiling.

The knot in my center loosened. I didn't know what dark force would escape when it unraveled completely. I tried not to think about the voice from last night, the voice of the other me. Yesterday, I would have called it anxiety. Yesterday, I would have said that my preoccupation with bad things happening to me was a tad self-absorbed. Today, though, I knew where that feeling came from.

It began in 1989, the day that I left New Jersey. It grew bigger each time I corrected myself to fit a new place: Oklahoma, the Church, high school, college. Every time I submitted to someone. It was all coming to a head now. It was her. It was

Mary Hall. It was my shadowy and coarse other self. The girl who lived in Marigold Court, who ran from wild dogs and was grateful for firemen and who hid in basements when her daddy played guitar in strange houses. She was the deep wrongness in me, the thing I feared would draw disaster to me like a tornado to a trailer park. I was not expecting to bargain the terms of my existence between my physical self and my psychic self. Mary Hall might have only existed in my mind for the past sixteen years, but she was more real than the person I had been pretending to be.

I was a clipping. I was a knockoff, the bastard version of the girl I was born to be.

In this fresh state of awareness I realized I hadn't cried in thirteen years. Not since Jacob left Oklahoma. I didn't cry when Mimi got sick, or when I left for college, not when I met Lisa, not when I said goodbye to her again. Not for things that any normal person would be affected by. Those things had made me sad, but I turned away from that sadness immediately, as if I had accidentally touched a hot stove.

Denial is a crooked crutch. When it's all you have, you don't see how it bends away from you, the way it makes each step longer and more tedious. When you're deep in reliance on such a twisted thing, you adjust yourself to accommodate it. You two coil together so tight that it becomes impossible to tell where you end and it begins. You have to break your own bones to get at it, break yourself up so you can be set straight. It's messy work best done alone, so you set right. So you don't grow your bones around some other crooked thing and have to break yourself up again.

So far I had avoided being rocked by the impacts of my life's turmoil by subconsciously shutting down my emotional centers. But in life, no one is spared, no one is let off the hook. Those buried sensations had to come out, be felt, addressed, and lived through.

I wish I could say I let it all out that night. All of the tears, all of the screams, all of the bullshit. But I didn't. I couldn't. It would take something much stronger to bring all that out of me. Still. By the time the sun rose the next morning, one thing had changed: I was no longer full of shit.

I moved out of the house on Forty-fourth Street for the final time. Maybe it looked like running away, but it felt like the right move. I could see the hurt and concern on Mimi and Granddad's faces as I dragged out my boxes of books and sweaters. I wanted to not hurt them. I wanted to take it back. But I couldn't do what I needed to do without hurting them. Hurting them was part of it. I needed to trust them to be hurt and not abandon me.

I drove west; needing to escape the gravitational pull of both of my families and anyone who knew them. I needed to wallow in uncertainty, without the balancing effects of religion or school, or friends, or family to cling to. If I was ever going to figure out who I was, I needed to be a stranger again.

Requiem

L os Angeles.
  I'd never seen the city before I moved in. The California in my mind was so sunny, so easy, so obvious. But it was far away from anyone or anything I knew and there wouldn't be any school, church, or parents to give me rules to follow.

My apartment was in Los Feliz. The neighborhood was named after a man who had been the mayor of Los Angeles when it was a pueblo under Mexican rule, but it also translated as "happy" in Spanish. It was nestled at the foot of Hollywood Hills and covered in palm trees; so it was easy to think the name came from the latter.

Los Angeles was a city full of transplants, of people searching for fame, glory, or inner peace. I wouldn't say I was entirely at home, but I no longer felt like the strangest person in the room. I found a job managing a restaurant in West Hollywood and made friends slowly. I was vigilant against my habit of absorbing people's gestures and sublimating my own thoughts. In the absence of other people to influence me, I slowly discovered the things I liked and didn't like. I was like a baby; everything was new.

For the first year in Los Feliz, all I owned was an air mattress and a table. And I was fine. I was pleasantly surprised to discover that the scrappiness I'd learned as a child in South Jersey was still part of my foundation; it hadn't died under the years of material comfort as I feared.

Other than my sisters, I'd never known anyone who had been adopted. In my first year in Los Angeles I met nearly a dozen. It was the first time I interacted with strangers who, in the middle of a banal conversation, used the words *birth parents*, *adoptive parents*, and described varying degrees of siblinghood with alacrity. In those moments I felt insignificant in a good way. Like the way you do when you look up at the sky on a clear night after a rain and you are so squashed under the enormity of so many stars that your little people problems don't seem like anything worth worrying about.

It was difficult for me to think about going back to ways that I had previously existed. High school reunions, college reunions, friends' weddings that would be full of people from my prior lives, were minefields. On the rare occasion I attended such things, I could feel myself contorting to fit their expectations of how I should behave, like the girl I had been before, and I loathed myself for it. But some reunions were inevitable.

I'd been living in Los Angeles for two years when I got the call from Granddad. "You have to come now. The doctors say this is it," he said.

I was in a cab to LAX before I hung up the phone.

Jacob picked me up in Dallas on his way up from Houston and we drove together into a massive ice storm. We arrived in Oklahoma City in time to grab Becca from the Will Rogers World Airport.

Granddad was in the room with Mimi when Jacob, Becca, and I arrived at the hospital. He wore a translucent fiber gown and plastic gloves over his light blue sweater. Mimi's chart showed that she had a staph infection on her skin at one point in her hospital stay, and the protocol required all of us to wear those things if we wanted to touch her.

"I don't see how it matters now," Granddad said, gently releasing Mimi's hand so he could hug Becca and me hello.

His eyes were rimmed in red and his sweater sagged at the elbows and belly. He must have lost fifteen pounds since I'd last seen him.

"Can I talk to her?" Jacob gestured to Mimi in the bed.

"Oh, sure, sure." Granddad pulled a gown and gloves from a box by the door.

My brother rested his gloved hands lightly on Mimi's left arm. He told her about his wife and his two young sons. "I'm sorry they won't get to meet you," he said. "You'd like them, they're good boys."

Listening to Jacob's words felt like an intrusion. But curiosity was more powerful than my sense of propriety. I needed to see it with my own eyes, what the act of letting go looked like. I was glad that there was someone older than me to go first. It would be my turn soon and I had no idea where I would begin.

There were too many things to say. For ten years I knew this day was coming. I'd had plenty of time to prepare. But so much of that decade had been chewed up by my attempts to figure out who I was, with retreating into the cocoon of the reunions with my sisters. I hadn't yet begun to unpack my relationship with Mimi. And now it was time. I would have to speak both sides of our conversation. As Mary, I would say that I was sorry for not being around more in her final years. Then I'd say Mimi's part—that she forgave me. Mimi would say that she was sorry she'd sent my brother away. And I would say that I forgave her, too. It was all so long ago.

Granddad hugged us goodbye and said he would be back in the morning to relieve us.

This would be harder for Becca and Granddad than for me. They loved Mimi, and it was obvious she loved them, too. Becca was losing her mother, a woman she adored and who adored her. What was I losing?

Mimi was a legend, a mentor, a monster, an artisan, an icon to me. I blamed her and hated her and was fascinated by her. But I also wanted to be like her. Strong and efficient, fierce and wise. I respected her and misunderstood her and didn't know her, not really.

Underneath everything I regretted and was sorry for, I was simultaneously stupidly, messily grateful. That she came to New Jersey that day in 1989, that she brought me to a place where I could play piano and sing in church and read books to her out loud in her basement workshop. That she told me I could leave even when she was sick, that she hadn't held me hostage when she could have. I couldn't remember if I told her thank you, or if I just thought it at her and hoped she'd picked up on it.

Did she love me? I had never been sure, and now I would never know. Those thoughts seemed picayune and cruel against the vast backdrop of life and death.

Jacob, Becca, and I spent the night with her at the hospital. I relied on the only thing that had never disappointed me: the words of other people. I started singing "Fly Me to the Moon," a song Mimi had played in the car often when I was a kid. Becca chimed in with the alto line and for a few moments—mere fragments of breath—we met in effortless harmony. The song joined me and my sister and brother and Mimi in a way we had never been before. A way we never would be again.

It was nine o'clock on New Year's morning when Granddad returned and my brother, sister, and I drove to the house on Forty-fourth Street to shower.

Mimi drew her final breath when we were on our way back to the hospital. Jolene was waiting for us in the lobby when we walked through the doors.

"Oh! Mary, she's gone. She just slipped away, just now." Jolene patted my shoulders with both of her hands, in a close approximation of a hug. That syllable "Oh!" always struck me. The surprise of it, the shock, the desperation, like a splash of ice-cold water on my face.

After the hospital arranged to transport Mimi to the funeral home, Granddad and I went to the church we had attended since I was ten years old. It was the Feast of the Solemnity of Mary, a holy day of obligation. Since I'd moved to Los Angeles I had been taking a break from the Church. But I couldn't let Granddad attend alone. He would be sitting in this pew alone every Sunday; I couldn't let him start today.

We sat in the fifth pew from the back on the left-hand side of the altar, the place he and Mimi had sat for eighteen years. Becca and Jacob stayed at the house on Forty-fourth Street to receive the people who dropped by with puddings and lasagnas. During the announcements at the end of service the priest advised the parish, "This morning we lost a longtime parishioner, Mimi King."

I had been expecting that; it's what was done before the Requiem Aeternam prayer.

But this time the priest took a detour. "You've all seen her, the tiny lady in the fifth pew on the left"——he gestured to the spot where Granddad and I stood—"accompanied by her husband Charles, whose steadfast care and devotion are the greatest testament of love that I have ever seen."

Granddad gripped the back of the pew in front of us and I reached over to cover his hands with mine; he hated anyone making a fuss. I felt his wedding band and his garnet ring against my palm. I was overwhelmed by that word, *love*, again, like I always had been, flattened under the weight of everything I did not understand.

The priest said:

Eternal rest grant unto her, O Lord.

And in a single baritone wave, the congregation responded:

And may perpetual light shine upon her.
May she rest in peace.
Amen.

After Mass, Granddad and I met Jolene at the funeral home. She wanted to curl Mimi's hair for the laying out. "I couldn't stand it if she didn't look like herself," Jolene said.

The funeral director set us up in a back room of the garage where they parked the limousine fleet. The floor and walls were concrete and the place was freezing. I stood to keep my blood flowing.

Mimi's body was laid on a steel table, covered with a sheet. Only her head poked out. Her face was made up with peach cheeks, pink lips. Flesh-colored paste covered the bruises where the oxygen mask had rubbed her skin raw. It was clear that Mimi was no longer present in this humanlike shell in front of us. The body on the table was just a body. It looked more like one of the dolls Mimi sculpted than a person.

I pulled a notepad out of my purse to begin the obituary. We didn't need to discuss it; Jolene and I knew it needed to be done and that we were the ones who would do it. We were Mimi's daughters, which made us sisters. I wasn't sure if Jolene would be a stepsister, or a half-sister, or both; I'd only ever acknowledged that relationship as a punch line.

"Mimi was the kind of person you'd want on your side," I brainstormed.

"You really think so?" Jolene snorted, nearly swallowing the hairpins in the corner of her mouth.

"I remember one time, when Mother and I lived behind the bar . . . she promised to drive a girlfriend to the hospital when she went into labor. The husband was overseas." Jolene combed a severe part with a rattail comb. "Well, the day came, and boy! The phone was just ringing off the hook and Mother was dead asleep. That woman took a cab to have her baby."

There was too much new information in that story. Mimi had lived behind a bar, had been a daytime sleeper, had flaked out on someone who needed her.

"I don't know why I'm doing this . . ." Jolene's hands dropped to her sides. "They have people to do this. It's just silly and sentimental. I've never set hair on a . . . like this."

Her fingers were red and the cuticles jagged from where she'd stabbed them with hairpins.

Later, I returned to the house on Forty-fourth Street and went straight to the bookcases in the hallway, to the drawers of mementos that Mimi never let me go through. I sat in the middle of the room with all the lights blazing and unearthed stacks of black-and-white photos, translucent birth certificates and marriage licenses. Photos of toddler Mimi with her hair in a blunt bowl cut rested on top of a 1945 portrait of Mimi with her hair ornately curlicued around her face. Underneath were photographs of the red-cheeked boys that she'd married before Granddad. By my count there had been at least three. She'd sat for a professional portrait every year, it seemed, from 1942 until she married Granddad in 1966. Her hair faded from raven-black to golden blond as the years progressed. Her dimples became less pronounced. She wasn't smiling in any of the pictures—though sometimes she smirked. Her face was always bare except for a swipe of lipstick, her eyebrows were always perfect. Most of the time her ears were covered. She hated her ears.

Is this what makes a person? A catalog of former surnames and peccadilloes? When I strung them together, what did I have? Mimi hated her ears and was married many times and one time she let her friend take a cab to the hospital and one time she taught me how to sew and one time she hated my brother even though he was just a kid. And she made dolls and loved dogs and she taught me to love books. I looked up to the empty air above me, as if I might find her hovering there, waiting to slap my hand and say, *A nosy person deserves whatever she finds out.*

The unabridged dictionary poked out from the top shelf and caught my eye. Granddad had special-ordered it along with an atlas the size of a sheet cake when Becca and I started middle school. It had been used when we were kids mostly to balance on our heads to prove which of us had the most excellent posture and superior neck strength. I pulled the dictionary onto my lap and flipped the pages until I found it.

LOVE [luhv] noun

The primary entry defined love as a intensely held affection for another person. The sort of connection a person would feel for a parent or a child. Which is what I always thought it meant. That was what I felt for Peggy when I was a child. Mimi was never what you would call warm or affectionate. Neither was I. But there was more. Below descriptions of sincere liking and genuine passion was the definition that stopped me cold. The last entry explained love as a need; a thing that is required in the course of development. The way plants need and profit from the sun. The way plants *love* the sun.

That was where I recognized us. I loved Mimi like a plant loved the sun. I couldn't help it. So what if we weren't the first definition, the purest form of the thing? A lesser-used form is no less true. Love wasn't just about affection. It was about nourishment. It was about showing up. She nourished me and I needed her. Of those two actions, Mimi definitely had the harder job. As much as I fought it, as much as I didn't want to feel it, I knew in that moment that I had loved her.

I realized, finally, that loving Mimi and Granddad was not a betrayal of Peggy or Jacob. Love was not finite. I did not have to earmark a special portion for each of them, balance it and keep it fair.

In the days after Mimi's death, I felt more like a child than I ever had in my entire life. I was like a baby, with no idea what I needed to make me comfortable, just fussing and reaching out until anyone reached back.

I gritted my teeth so much over the next twenty-four hours that I cracked a filling in my left molar. My childhood dentist came back early from his holiday to replace it for me.

Over the next two days, every demonstration of kindness destroyed me. Girls I hadn't seen since high school came to the wake and I felt as if my skin had cracked open. Off-duty police officers on motorcycles stopped traffic so we could drive to the cemetery in one unimpeded line, and my bones ached for them riding in the cold. The cemetery was one solid sheet of ice, but blankets were laid on the chairs by the casket as if draped there by elves. I was humbled into muteness by the time we returned to the church for the post-funeral supper.

The ladies of the Altar Society quietly milled around the kitchen of the parish hall; they were well versed in ministering to mourners. A Filipina woman in thick glasses placed the final platter on the buffet table as we removed our ice-crusted coats. The simple table was laden with those comforting things that spell affection in the plains: biscuits, brownies, sweet tea, macaroni casserole, fried chicken.

At the end of the dinner, the Filipina woman wrapped the leftovers in foil and pressed them into my hands. She said, "Peace be with you," as she tied a scarf around her feathered pixie cut and prepared to head into the cold. I had to turn my face to the wall to bear the weight of all that goodness.

Meeting Lesley

I met the last of my lost sisters, Lesley, at Jacob's long-postponed Real Wedding. It was in Houston, Texas, on a hot February weekend in 2011. Jacob would ship out for his last tour in Iraq two days later. He and his wife had been married for five years, but they said their original vows in a stuffy room on an air base in Germany and they'd always said they'd have a do-over later, for the family. Jacob's three tours in Iraq and the births of their two sons kept pushing back the main event. But it was finally here.

As I waited to board my flight at the Los Angeles International Airport it struck me that all the important moments in my life involved flying or driving. Never home and never not-home, always some in-between place. I liked the way the journey provided parentheses. It buffered my moments with my family from the ordinary business of life.

It was sunny when I landed in Texas. The people waiting in baggage claim for their loved ones wore shorts. I scanned the crowd for my brother, but he wasn't there yet. So I stepped outside and called his cell phone. For a brief second I stood in the sunshine and it was just me and the concrete under my feet and the placid ringing in my ear and it was calm.

Then Jacob answered on the other end of the line and I was filled with the chaos of voices piling up in the backseat of a car I could not yet see but knew was close.

"The friggin' security guys made me keep circling. So I'm circling."

Underneath his words voices chimed my name at different pitches and in their own rhythms. *Mary Mary Mary*, like a canon. I smiled and soaked it in.

Jacob had traded his sedan for a black SUV, a Texas-sized thing that glistened like a beetle's shell in the sunlight. As he glided to the curb I could see that my brother, as always, left the front passenger seat for me. It was my birthright. I could see my sisters' faces through the windshield—Becca, Rebekah, Meghan, and Lesley. Lisa had just re-enrolled in college and couldn't afford to make the trip this time. Even for such a big event we couldn't manage to get all seven of us in the same place at the same time. I wondered if we ever would.

Lesley was in the way-backseat, squeezed between Becca and Meghan. Her butter-blond bobbed hair perfectly framed the blue eyes that took up most of her facial real estate.

"Hey, sis," she said. Like she'd been saying it for years. Her voice had the same growl as Peggy's. She was twenty-one years old. The same age Peggy was when Jacob was born. She was so young.

"That's not her natural hair color," Meghan pointed out to me.

"It's *fashion*," Lesley corrected.

Lesley had two crystal studs embedded into her clavicle. My eyes kept darting down to her chest, trying to figure out how that could work.

"They're dermals," Lesley said, clearly accustomed to the attention. "They're anchored in there good, don't worry."

"Fashion?" I asked.

"Yeah, fashion," she agreed and, to my surprise, moved seamlessly into a stream-of-consciousness slam-poetry-style rap. "You know it's fa-shion. You can't be crashin' in my party looking like a smarty, if you wanna sip on my Bacardi you got to have. The. Look."

Becca and Rebekah howled in the middle seat.

"You should know that she raps as much as she speaks like a normal person," Meghan advised.

"Girl, you're jealous," Lesley said with a smile.

Lesley had Becca's face. Her whole face. The cheeks, the nose, the lips, the chin, it was all there. And she had the same disarming sincerity about her that had always made people want to befriend Becca.

We drove to Jacob's in-laws' giant stone house in the Houston suburbs.

When I arrived, Granddad and Peggy were sitting side by side on the back porch smiling for family photos with Jacob's sons. These brown-eyed toddlers were Peggy's grandchildren, Granddad's great-grandchildren. It seemed that the mere passage of time had wrought more grace on all of us than I thought was possible.

Our sister-in-law had invited all of us to be part of the bridal party. It wasn't that she needed us—she already had five bridesmaids without us—but it was a gesture of inclusion and we all accepted.

The place bustled with Katy's parents' friends, Katy's sister and brother, the rest of the wedding party. I could tell that they all knew our story; they had prepared faces for us to see. They sustained eye contact, blinked little; as if constantly reminding themselves they were not looking at ghosts, but real people.

"If one more person smiles at me, I'm gonna need a drink," Becca whispered to me.

I watched my sisters as we sat in the kitchen alongside Peggy and Katy, shearing roses and wrapping them in floral tape. I remembered what Meghan said the night we met her: *Lesley always said that she felt like she had a piece missing.* This youngest sister had sensed our existence before she even had proof she was adopted. Was that hole a memory of Jacob, Becca, and I that fateful summer of 1989, in the Camden apartment where she was conceived? Had she absorbed our voices the way doctors say developing babies sense light and music through the womb?

The hotel that night was like summer camp. Rebekah, Meghan, Lesley, and I gathered in Becca's room because the rooms around her were empty; we could be as loud as we wanted. Lesley and Becca brought out their guitars and faced one another on ottomans. I sat on the floor, looking up at them as their freckled arms strummed in unison and their faces were raised to the ceiling like wolves howling at the moon.

They were the bright shadow of Michael and Mac, men none of us had ever really known. In this room I was the only one who held this earlier image of the men who had come before us, the spark of the tragedy that started our split all those years ago. I wondered what Peggy would feel if she were in this room right now.

Rebekah sat on the floor beside me, bobbing her head in time to the music. The wall behind our backs vibrated with sound. When the music paused, she leaned her head on my shoulder and asked, "Do you think we're cursed?"

I dug deep into the corners of my brain to answer her. I wanted to say that I could see why she thought we might be; our family tree cast a lot of deep shadows. It seemed every one of us had a tendency to beeline to rock bottom. But then, once we hit it, hadn't we bounced? And wasn't it improbable, miraculous even, that we had all found one another? Wasn't it bizarrely amazing that we had searched and had been found?

I wanted to tell her all these things, but I was overcome with the feeling that I didn't need to say anything; everyone around me already *got* it. So as I leaned my cheek on Rebekah's head I thought my thoughts into that dim Houston hotel room and I was certain that my sisters understood. I was certain that Peggy and Michael and Lisa and Mimi and Granddad, wherever they were, understood, too.

All I said was, "Not anymore."

My sisters and I were scheduled to meet the other bridesmaids for hair and makeup at six-thirty in the morning. We had coffee instead of sleep. "It's what we always do," Becca told Lesley as we filled enormous paper cups in the hotel breakfast bar. I smiled. We were a "we" now. We had things that we always did.

My sisters and I piled into a rented silver sedan; Becca drove and Meghan sat beside her. Rebekah, Lesley, and I squeezed into the backseat. The floor at our feet was cluttered with strappy shoes, tins of hair spray, gum wrappers. We passed a travel-sized bottle of Listerine between us, swishing the burning liquid around our teeth and spitting out the window. Our dresses were plastic-wrapped and laid securely in the trunk where we couldn't wreck them. It was barely light outside, but already waves shimmered on the pavement ahead of us like ghosts, promises of heat to come. There wasn't a single other soul on the wide expanse of blacktop.

A song played low on the radio as we took in the sun rising over the flat Texas horizon. It didn't matter how we had gotten here, what had gone right or wrong in our lives. In that moment, we were a world unto ourselves. We were complete.

Acknowledgments

I must thank my agent, Lisa Gallagher. Your counsel, humor, and endless enthusiasm are blessings that I am constantly humbled to receive.

To my editor Jill Bialosky and everyone at Norton—Thank you for your patience and guidance. You made it possible for there to be a place in this world where my siblings and I can be together, in some small way, forever.

Thank you to Peter Balakian, Franz Wisner, Jennifer Vanderbes, Sarah Bay-Cheng, and Kseniya Melnik; without your early encouragement I might have lacked the guts to continue.

To my incredible friend Kimberlee Soo, thank you for sharing your infallible reflex for truth, for those hours of revision over coffee and conversation; you taught me a master class in generosity and I hope that someday I will have the opportunity to repay it.

To my dear family—Mom and Granddad, Jacob, Becca, Lisa, Rebekah, Meghan, and Lesley—it is said there is a blessing in each trial and you have all been that for me. Having you in my life is the greatest gift that I will ever know. Thank you for understanding that it is important to describe the shadows as well as the light, and for graciously allowing me to tell pieces of your stories where they overlapped with mine.

To the families who raised my sisters—we may not know one another well, or at all, but I cannot thank you enough for loving my sisters, for supporting them, and sharing them with my family, even when it is has been difficult.

Actually, especially when it has been difficult.

I am deeply indebted to my Mimi who introduced me to my greatest love, this wild, wonderful world of words. And to Louisa May Alcott, Laura Ingalls Wilder, Charlotte and Emily Bronte, whose books were always there when I needed a story to disappear into.

And finally, to Brian; thank you for accompanying me on this adventure, for your unfailing support in writing and in life, for everything. I am full of quantum you.